For my wonderful wife and
travelling companion, Louella

ISBN 978-1-911187-84-4

First published by Connell Publishing 2018

Cover illustration @NatBasil/Shuttercock

Design: Ben Brannan
Typesetting: Brian Scrivener
Picture research: Harry Deniston
Edited by Jolyon Connell

Printed in Spain

ALL YOU NEED TO KNOW....

THE GREATEST EXPLORERS

BY ROBIN HANBURY-TENISON

CONTENTS

INTRODUCTION

The achievements of the world's greatest explorers have inspired me all my life. We live in a world where pessimism is rife and where big decisions about the way the planet should be run are often based on a dangerously narrow life experience. And there is so much we can learn from the exploits and discoveries of the extraordinary, bold risk-takers who over hundreds of years have sought to find out about our world and to pass on their knowledge: in a sense we should all, and constantly, be trying to ape them: to broaden our experience, to understand how others live and think.

Visiting other countries not as a consumer or tourist but to learn, as explorers do, is a good way of curbing first-world arrogance as well as first-world ignorance. By putting ourselves under trying conditions on difficult and dangerous journeys we can learn how to deal with anxiety, pressure and the demands of leadership. We can learn resourcefulness and other vital human skills that cannot easily be acquired by staying at home and watching television.

In this book I will tell the stories of the very greatest explorers and their, in some cases, quite staggering achievements. I begin – as is only fitting – with the so-called 'Father of History' himself, Herotodus, and I end, less predictably perhaps, with the extraordinary contemporary investigator of rainforests, Meg Lowman, who in the course of hundreds of hours suspended in canopies at the top of trees has been bitten by innumerable insects, most still unknown to science.

In between I tell the stories of a succession of great adventurers, and of the insatiable curiosity that drove them either west, like the Irish monk St Brendan, or east, as in the tremendous journeys of Ibn Battuta and Marco Polo. They're a mixed bunch, of course, the great explorers, and some are responsible for massacres and other terrible crimes. While the great 'discoverers of new worlds' like Columbus and Vasco da Gama, were driven largely by the thrill of finding out what lay beyond the known world, and the great African explorers, like David Livingstone, by missionary zeal, others, like the Portuguese adventurers Cortez and Pizarro were vastly less attractive figures, driven more by a lust for conquest and the acquisition of territory, or gold, than by noble or uplifting motives. But my aim in this book is not to pass judgement, but to tell their stories. And whatever it was that drove them, however wicked some of them may appear to be – indeed were – they are linked by one quality which is common to all, without exception: an extraordinary, and in some cases almost unbelievable, physical courage.

HERODOTUS 450BC

Often described as the 'Father of History', Herodotus of Halicarnassus was born in about 484BC. Fearless, adventurous and indefatigable, he lived through the golden age of ancient Greece, numbering among his contemporaries Pericles, Socrates, Sophocles and Thucydides. What makes him stand out from that august crowd was the legacy he left in the form of the world's first prose epic. His *Histories*, written in an era when poetry was the ultimate form of literary expression, was twice as long as Homer's *Iliad*. It was, at the time, by far the world's longest volume and has remained a compelling literary voyage of discovery to this day.

The early part of the *Histories* is taken up with chronicling the cataclysmic Greek wars against the Persians from the 6th century BC, and the invasions of Persian emperors and kings – up to and including the heroics of King Leonidas's Spartans at Thermopylae in the early 5th century BC. As an explorer, however, Herodotus comes into his own when he describes sailing up the Nile as far as the rushing waters of the first rapids.

Here his skills as travel writer, pioneering geographer and anthropologist are fully revealed. Describing how crocodiles are hunted on Elephantine, an island on the Nile, he writes:

> a hook is baited with the back of a pig, and set to float in the middle of the river; meanwhile, on the riverbank, the hunter has a real live pig, which he wallops. The crocodile, hearing the squeals, makes a rush in the direction of the noise, comes across the bait, gulps it down – and in he is hauled. Once the crocodile has been landed, the first thing the hunter does is to smear mud all over his eyes. Only manage this, and the remaining stages of the crocodile's capture can easily be completed; fail to do it, and there will be trouble.

By contrast, he tells of their religious significance around Thebes:

> In these places they keep one particular crocodile, which they tame, putting rings of glass or gold into its ears and bracelet round its front feet, giving it special food and ceremonial offerings. In fact, while these creatures are alive they treat them with every kindness, and when they die, they embalm them and bury them in sacred tombs.

He recounts, too, the weird sexual customs of those among whom he travels. In Babylon, for example, he writes that women had to serve Mulissu, the goddess of love, as prostitutes.

> There is one custom amongst these people which is wholly shameful: every woman who is native of the country must once in her life go and sit in the temple of Aphrodite and

A statue of Herodotus in Vienna

there give herself to a strange man... Once a woman has taken her seat she is not allowed to go home until a man has thrown her a silver coin into her lap and taken her outside to lie with her.

But Herodotus was far from just a storyteller. He took soundings of the Nile's depth and speculated on the relationship between the river and the Red Sea, recognising the contribution of the colossal alluvial deposits which provided Egypt with her wealth and which he named 'the gift of the Nile'. This was geology 2,000 years before the term was invented.

He describes, too, all the already ancient monuments he sees along the way, and the strange practices, such as mummification, which were still being performed, as well as the burial rituals, the sacrifices and the pyramids, some of those he saw being more than 2,500 years old: in other words already built more years before *his* time than he lived before *ours*. One of his tales concerns Cheops, an Egyptian king who ordered the building of an 800ft high burial chamber for himself, a project which took 20 years to complete. To raise the money, says Herodotus, Cheops forced his own daughter into a brothel. "She charged the rate set by her father but also asked each of her clients to donate a single stone, and with these stones a pyramid was built, the middle of the three which stand in front of the Great Pyramid."

Herodotus's research, unparalleled in its scope and detail, remained the best source of knowledge of ancient Egypt until the 19th century AD. It is true that he has often been criticised for embellishing the truth – and called the 'Father of Lies' as well as the 'Father of History'. Yet even if we take some of his tales about flying snakes and gold-digging ants with a pinch of salt he has much to teach us. He was the first to observe and record a major clash of civilisations: that between the Eastern Persians and the Western Greeks, who were at that time bringing to birth the first democracy. He observed and understood the irreconcilable differences between the empires with their different value systems and he wrote, most presciently: "Everyone without exception believes his own native customs, and the religion he was brought up in, to be the best." This is as relevant and as widely unrecognised today as it was then.

ST BRENDAN OF CLONFERT 484-C.577 & LEIF ERICSSON C.970-C.1020

In the 6th century AD St Brendan and seventeen Irish monks are said to have set sail in a leather boat from an inlet in County Kerry in search of paradise and solitude. It seems likely that they did reach Iceland and possible that they may even have made landfall in America. The ancient Irish text known as the *Navigatio* of St Brendan is curiously accurate about places they would have reached on the way, such as Iceland and Greenland.

In the late 1970s, Tim Severin, the great modern maritime explorer, built a replica boat from 49 ox-hides and succeeded in reaching Newfoundland in 50 days, thus proving that it could have happened. There were certainly Irish monks living in Ice-land by the 8th century, though two hundred years later they were driven out by the Norsemen, who brought their families and ani-mals with them to settle there.

By this time – the late 10th century – Norsemen had also set-tled in Greenland, among them (and possibly one of the first) being a Viking king known as Eric the Red. By now, too, intrepid sailors were reporting land even further west, and in about the year 1000, Leif Ericsson, son of Eric the Red, crossed the Davis Strait between Greenland and Labrador before sailing along an increasingly forested coast until well south of the southern tip of Greenland.

He and his 35 companions landed at a place they called Mark-land, which means Wood Land, in northern Newfoundland, then explored inland and along the coast. They wintered – and built a house – where a river flowed out of a lake. Here they caught many salmon, bigger than any they had seen before, and even gathered wild grapes, naming the place Vinland. After what proved to be a mild winter – and having become the first Europeans we know of to have landed in continental North America – they loaded up their boat with timber and sailed with a good wind back to Greenland.

Leif Ericsson never returned, but others did, including his brother, who was killed in a skirmish with local people, perhaps the ancestors of the Chippewa or Ojibwe Indians. There were other voyages, many in search of timber, but there were no per-manent settlements, few records were kept and the Norse did not broadcast their discoveries. Basque and Breton fishermen visiting the vast cod fishing banks off the Newfoundland coast may have made accidental contact with America as well, but several hundred years were to pass before the existence of a continent across the Atlantic was to be proved.

MARCO POLO C.1254-1324

In 1271, aged only 17, Marco Polo set off from Venice on a journey to China which was to last for 23 years. He was accompanying his father and uncle, Venetian traders, who had only returned from a previous ten-year journey two years before. They had carried back with them a letter to the Pope from Kublai Khan, the Great Khan, who ruled Cathay, as China was then known, which he had recently conquered. The letter invited 100 learned men to visit China and requested oil from the lamp in the Church of the Holy Sepulchre in Jerusalem.

Carrying the oil and letters from the Pope, the Italian travellers took three and a half years to reach the Great Khan's winter palace and capital, Cambaluc (Beijing). Their route took them through Georgia and Armenia, then south to the Persian Gulf at Hormuz where they planned to take ship to China; but they found the ships there "wretched affairs... only stitched together

A portrait of Marco Polo in Tartar costume

with twine made from the husk of the Indian nut". And so they decided to travel overland instead, going through Afghanistan, over the Pamirs, "the highest place in the world", and on along the Silk Road through the Taklamakan and Gobi Deserts.

During the next 16 years, Marco Polo became a favourite of Kublai Khan. A gifted linguist, he was sent on special missions abroad to Burma and India, as well as travelling widely inside China itself. He was made an official of the Privy Council by the Emperor and, for three years, served as a tax inspector in Yan-zhou. His glowing description of one of the palaces later inspired Coleridge to write his poem about Kublai Khan's "stately pleasure dome" in Xanadu (Shangdu).

The Polos returned by sea, escorting a Mongol princess sent to marry a Persian prince, and then by land and sea by way of Tre-bizond and Constantinople. After two years they finally reached Venice again in 1295.

Imprisoned by the Genoese in 1298 as the result of a brief war with Venice, Marco Polo found himself sharing a cell with a French romance writer called Rustichello, to whom he told the long story of all his adventures and the sights he had seen. The resulting book, *Travels*, or *A Description of the World*, amazed everyone who read it and has been the subject of much speculation ever since. It revealed that there was a country far to the east which was culturally and materially well in advance of the Christian Mediterranean world. Polo described a postal service that could deliver a letter by courier 300 miles in a day; coal, "a stone that burned"; and asbestos, "a cloth that wouldn't". All these and many other things he saw and told of were not yet known in the west.

Many thought it was all lies, which is hardly surprising given that some of his tales seemed scarcely plausible to people in Europe – of mountains so high that there were no birds on them; of deserts so hot they turned dead bodies to dust; of a country (India) where cows were sacred; of an island (Sumatra) where peo-

A miniature from 'The Travels of Marco Polo', originally published in the 13th century, during his lifetime

ple ate each other; of a potentate, the Great Khan, so rich and magnificent that he clothed his nobles "in bejewelled garments", and had five thousand elephants decked out in gold cloth and "ten thousand falconers". But though many doubted his tales, there is no doubt that Marco Polo challenged the accepted order of the universe, as it was seen from Christian Europe. His voyage also, ironically, inspired Christopher Columbus 200 years later, to seek a western passage to Cathay, carrying with him his own heavily annotated copy of *Travels*.

IBN BATTUTA 1304-68

Thirty years after Marco Polo returned from his travels, a 21-year-old Moroccan Muslim born in Tangier set out alone on a donkey on what has been called the greatest journey of all time. It started as a conventional *Hajj*, the pilgrimage to Mecca every Muslim is expected to make once in his or her lifetime, only Ibn Battuta just kept travelling. During the next 24 years he went halfway round the world visiting every Muslim country and many others, determined never to venture down the same road more than once.

By August 1326, 14 months after leaving Tangier, he was in Damascus where the Black Death, a terrible pandemic which was to rage across Europe had recently arrived. He witnessed an extraordinary scene when the people

went out together on foot, holding Korans in their hands…
The procession was joined by the entire population of the

town, men and women, small and large; the Jews came with their Book of the Law and the Christians with their Gospel, all of them with their women and children. The whole concourse, weeping and supplicating and seeking the favour of God through His Books and His Prophets, made their way to the Mosque of the Footprints [of Moses], and there they remained in supplication and invocation.

This is an early example of ecumenical worship which seems to have worked, as Battuta claims that only 2,000 people died that day, whereas in Egypt tens of thousands were dying.

After finally reaching Mecca, he went south along the coast of Africa as far as Mombassa before going back north to Constantinople, where the Emperor presented him with a horse, and then east to India, where he saw yogis performing magic tricks and Hindu wives practising *suttee* by climbing on to their husbands' funeral pyres. He had many adventures on the way to China, including being shipwrecked and nearly executed, but once there he saw more of the wonders described by Marco Polo, such as coal and paper money, which astonished him.

Their buying and selling is carried on exclusively by means of pieces of paper... When these notes become torn by handling, one takes them to an office, corresponding to our mint, and receives their equivalent in new notes on delivering up the old ones.

It would be almost 500 years before this practice caught on in Europe.

He returned in triumph to Morocco in 1349 and then made another journey south to Timbuktu and back across the central Sahara desert. He caused great confusion for subsequent explorers by identifying the Niger as the Nile and assuming it continued to flow eastwards as far as Egypt. However, he was the first explorer to cross the whole of Asia and bring back a description, complete with a remarkably accurate system of measuring distance. His work has been called the precursor of scientific geography.

ZHENG HE, THE GRAND EUNUCH 1371-1435

For most of its history China, though more inventive and further advanced than the west in many ways, has been staunchly isolationist, uninterested in overseas exploration or conquest – except of its near neighbours. In the early years of the Ming Dynasty, however, a new emperor, Yongle, came to the throne and decided to assert Chinese suzerainty over the barbarian lands beyond the sea. In 1405, he assembled the greatest armada the world had ever seen, or was to see until the First World War. It consisted of 63 ocean-going junks, some with nine masts and ten times as big as Columbus's *Santa Maria*, which would not be built for another 85 years. The vessels were some of the largest sail-powered wooden ships in human history.

Yongle put in charge of this fleet a Muslim eunuch, Zheng He, who was to undertake seven rare voyages of exploration, reaching as far west as Arabia and the coast of Africa and south through today's Indonesia, perhaps even as far as Australia. Zheng He's captains navigated by compass, which had been invented by the Chinese as early as the 8th century AD and was being used by them centuries before its general use in Europe. They burnt incense sticks to measure time and had developed a sophisticated navigation system based on a rectangular grid. It has been calculated that Zheng He sailed over 50,000 kilometres and visited 35 countries but, in sharp contrast to the European maritime expeditions of the next three centuries, his voyages were primarily undertaken for diplomatic and commercial reasons.

His ships carried with them a vast cargo of porcelain, silk and lacquer ware for trade, China's aim being to make friends and allies in the wider world. And they brought back an enormous amount of treasure collected along the way: rhinoceros horn, ivory, tortoiseshell, rare woods, incense, spices, medicines, pearls and precious stones. The strangest and most admired object was a live giraffe sent by the Sultan of Malindi, which was treated as a grand and auspicious omen when it reached the Forbidden City (the network of palaces at the heart of what is now Beijing).

The fleet, manned by 28,000 sailors, was very heavily armed and must have impressed and terrified those who saw it arrive, so that almost no one questioned the news that they were now vassals of the Chinese emperor. (Almost the only conflict to trouble Zeng He was with a pirate.) China could easily have become a great colonial empire, but by the time he returned from his final voyage in 1433, to die soon afterwards, there was a new emperor on the throne. China withdrew into itself once more, forbidding foreign voyages. Only today is it flexing its muscles again.

CHRISTOPHER COLUMBUS 1451-1506

Christopher Columbus was the man who revealed the exist-ence of America to Europe, even if he probably wasn't the first European to get there. The son of a weaver from Genoa in Italy, he spent eight years trying to confirm his belief that the world was round, consulting other like-minded people and creat-ing his own map of the world. This, while broadly accurate, made it about a quarter too small, convincing him that the westward route to Asia was much shorter than it really is.

Determined to prove he was right, he eventually – through charm and perseverance – convinced Queen Isabella of Spain to back him. She granted him the titles of Admiral of the Ocean Sea, Governor General and Viceroy of any lands he might dis-cover. This enabled him to raise finance from a consortium and, on the morning of 3 August 1492, he set sail in three caravels, *Niña, Pinta* and *Santa Maria*, from Palos in southern Spain. The ships stopped briefly in the Canaries and then sailed west into the unknown on 6 September.

On 12 October, after what was perhaps the longest period any European ship had spent out of sight of land – including a time becalmed in the Sargasso Sea and with his crews in open revolt – his look-out spotted a coastline. It was a still unidentified island in the Bahamas, which he named San Salvador.

When we stepped ashore we saw fine green trees, streams everywhere and different kinds of fruit... Soon many of the islanders gathered round us.

Convinced he had arrived in 'the Indies', the name then commonly given to Asia, Columbus called the people 'Indians'.

...wishing them to look on us with friendship I gave some of them red bonnets and glass beads which they hung round their necks, and many other things of small value, at which they were so delighted and eager to please us that we could not believe it. Later they swam out to the boats to bring us parrots and balls of cotton thread and darts and many other things, exchanging them for such objects as glass beads and hawk bells. They took eagerly and gave willingly whatever they had.

This promising relationship, as happens so often when remote peoples meet outsiders, lasted all too short a time. Soon the colonists' obsession with gold got the better of them; they quickly noticed that many of the Indians they met were wearing gold, and the discovery led to the ruthless exploitation of the island on which they had landed, just as the pursuit of gold led to the destruction

Christopher Columbus, who was convinced the world was round

A painting of Columbus landing in the West Indies by John Vanderlyn (1775-1852)

of innumerable other societies. The genocidal behaviour of those who followed Columbus caused great suffering and many deaths, but it was the European diseases they brought with them, such as smallpox, which did the greatest damage, wiping out as much as 80-90 per cent of the indigenous inhabitants in North America over the following century.

In the meantime, though, Columbus returned in triumph to Spain and processed through the streets with six naked captive Indians, each carrying a brightly coloured parrot in a cage.

He made three more voyages across the Atlantic, landing on the mainland of South America for the first time in 1496. He sighted, visited and named a great many of the Caribbean islands, from Cuba, Jamaica and Puerto Rico down to Trinidad and Tobago and the mainland shores of what are today Nicaragua, Costa Rica and Honduras. As a direct result of his discoveries, Spain was able to negotiate the Treaty of Tordesillas in which Pope Alexander VI decreed that all unclaimed territories to the east of an imaginary line 370 leagues west of Cape Verde would henceforth be Portuguese (hence Brazil), while all to the line's west (such as Mexico, Colombia and Peru) would be given to Spain.

His later life was marred by controversy. Appointed Viceroy and Governor of the Indies he was eventually summoned back to Spain amidst accusations of incompetence, tyranny and cruelty. He died in 1506 aged only 54, not poor, as he had brought back at least one shipload of gold, but disgraced and disillusioned. He never recognised the truth about where he had been.

VASCO DA GAMA 1469 – 1524

On 8 July 1497, more than a year before Columbus set out on his third voyage, a fleet of four ships left Lisbon on a journey that was to change forever relations between Europe and Asia. The commander was Vasco da Gama, an unknown Portuguese knight. A previous expedition to southern Africa by his fellow countryman Bartolomeu Dias had established that there was a circular wind system with westerlies which would carry ships around the Cape of Good Hope. As a result da Gama and his ships made good speed and he and his crew became the first Europeans to sail up the east African coast.

Contact with the indigenous populations was largely benign until they reached Mozambique and met Muslim Arabs. Once it was discovered the new arrivals were Christians, they were attacked and one of their ships was sunk. The remaining three managed to reach Mombasa where the travellers found more trouble and had to fight off a determined night attack. But a week later, at Malindi, they encountered a friendly regent or "sheik". The Sheik of Malindi had no time for the ruler in Mombasa, who he saw as a rival; he allowed the Portuguese to reprovision and, best of all, provided them with a skilled pilot. In 23 days, sailing with favourable monsoon winds, da Gama's ships crossed the Arabian Sea and arrived off the Malabar coast in southern India on 20 May 1498.

The coming of the Portuguese and the other Europeans who followed in their wake was to change the Indian subcontinent dramatically – and permanently. On this first visit, though, da Gama stayed only three months before, against the advice of his pilot, setting sail back to Africa in the absence of the vital monsoon winds. It was a mistake. In a deadly passage lasting just under three months, the Portuguese lost to scurvy more than 60 men, or nearly half of those who died on the entire voyage. When the remaining two ships reached Portugal just 44 of the original 175 were still alive.

The voyage had taken two years and they had sailed 23,000 nautical miles, greater than the distance around the world at the equator. They had achieved what only decades earlier had been considered impossible. The Portuguese king profited immensely from the insatiable demand for spices – a demand which had been stimulated by their new abundance through regular trade with the east. Production there rose dramatically, while the price in Europe actually increased threefold.

The epic voyage of da Gama is arguably the most significant in human history, as it brought about the first direct meeting between the west and the east since Alexander the Great, and from it came permanent contact and interaction. The consequences were mixed: Europe's superior technology weapons were spread across the world. So were Christianity and western culture, reaching many distant lands. But the conflict between Christians

Vasco da Gama, painted by Antonio Manuel da Fonseca

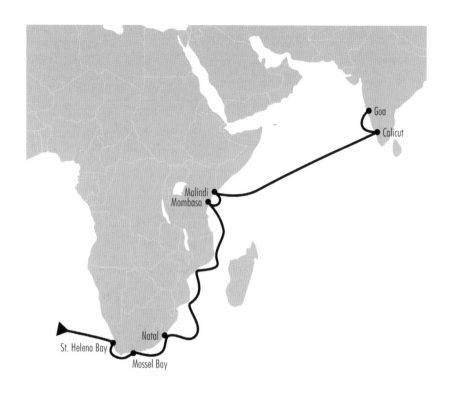

Vasco da Gama's epic voyage was arguably the most significant in human history.

and Muslims which this contact renewed, following the last Crusade, more than 200 years before, led to tensions which have never been resolved.

FERDINAND MAGELLAN 1480-1521

It was Magellan who first actually proved that the world was round, although he failed to go right round it himself. A Portuguese navigator, he was appointed captain-general of a fleet of five ships and 241 men and sent by the king of Spain in 1519 to explore a new route westward to the East Indies. This was the ultimate strategic goal for Spain, as Portugal had the monopoly on the route east and the fabulously rich spice islands as a result of Vasco da Gama's success in reaching India via the Cape of Good Hope. If it could be proved that they could be reached by sailing *west*, then Spain would have a claim on them.

After eight months, while off the coast of Brazil – heading south and seeking a way through to the ocean he knew must lie beyond to the west – Magellan had a mutiny on his hands. He put it down

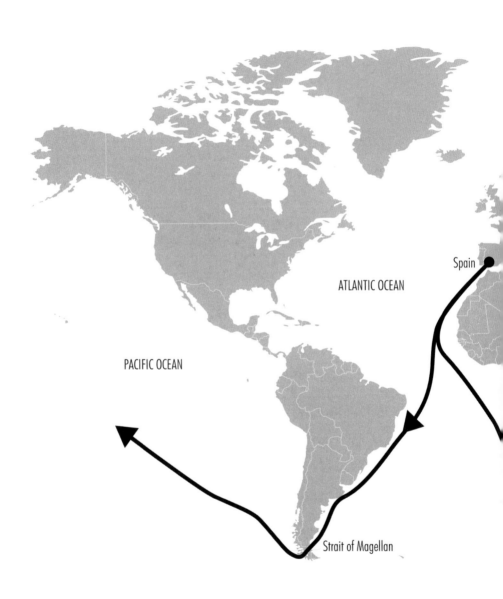

ATLANTIC OCEAN

PACIFIC OCEAN

Spain

Strait of Magellan

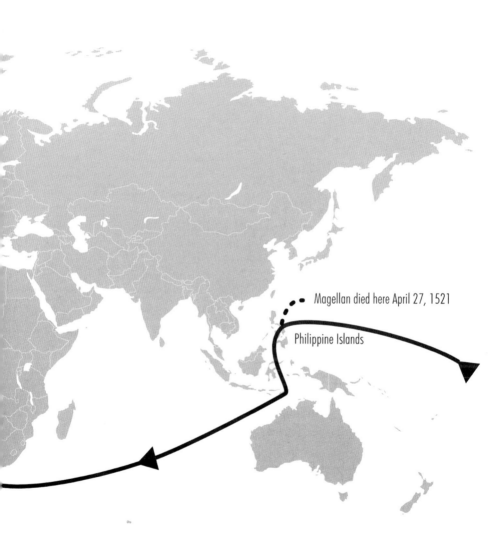

Magellan died here April 27, 1521

Philippine Islands

Magellan's voyage

ruthlessly, executing some of the ringleaders and marooning others on land. By October 1529, his small flotilla, now down to four ships – one had been wrecked – entered the tortuous and wind-swept channels of what is today called the Strait of Magellan and spent a fraught month seeking a way through the maze of water between snow-capped mountains.

During these weeks he lost another of his ships: her captain, fed up after months at sea, decided to escape; he turned his vessel round and ran for home carrying vital stores. But at last the three remaining craft, now manned by 200 men, burst out of the western end of the strait and arrived in a serene and tranquil sea. Magellan broke down and wept, declaring that from henceforth it would be known as the Pacific Ocean.

He now believed, wrongly, that the fabled spice islands were only a few days' sailing away. This was because his charts were based on Ptolemy's calculations of the 2nd century AD, which under-estimated the circumference of the earth by 6,835 miles. In fact, he and his crew had just entered the largest ocean in the world, containing more than half the water on the earth's surface and into which all the world's continents could fit. For more than three and a half months his ships crawled across this immense body of water, running out of food and water and suffering increasingly from scurvy.

> On Wednesday the twenty-eighth of November, one thou-
> sand five hundred and twenty, we issued forth from the
> said strait and entered the Pacific Sea, where we remained
> three months and twenty days without taking on board
> provisions or any other refreshments, and we ate only old
> biscuits turned to powder, all full of worms and stinking of
> the urine which the rats had made on it, having eaten the
> good. And we drank water impure and yellow. We ate also
> ox-hides which were very hard because of the sun, rain, and

Magellan: gave the Pacific Ocean its name

wind. And we left them four or five days in the sea, then laid them for a short time on embers, and so we ate them. And of the rats, which were sold for half an écu apiece [nearly a week's pay for a seaman], some of us could not get enough.… But above all the other misfortunes the following was the worst. The gums of both the lower and upper teeth of some of our men swelled, so that they could not eat under any circumstances and therefore died.

The symptoms he was describing were those of scurvy.

The landfall he and his men eventually made – after missing many Pacific islands close to which they must have sailed – was Guam, where finally they found food and water. From there it was but a short hop – by previous standards – to the Philippines, which they claimed for Spain. For a month the ships sailed among the islands enjoying good food and welcomed by friendly locals. Then disaster struck. Magellan offered to help a local chief on Cebú defeat an enemy on the neighbouring island of Mactan. But he miscalculated and found that he was facing 1,500 well-trained, fierce warriors. Magellan was killed and hacked to pieces, as were eight of his men. The rest fled back to the ships.

The remaining 115 men scuttled one ship, because they were now too short-handed to sail all three, and then spent six months sailing round the Moluccas collecting spices. The crew of one of the two remaining ships were imprisoned by the Portuguese but, eventually, the last ship, the 85-ton *Victoria*, captained by Sebastian d'Elcano and with only 18 surviving crew, made it back to Spain to a heroes' welcome almost exactly three years after the armada set out – and having proved conclusively that the earth was round.

The captain was presented by the king of Spain with a jewelled globe inscribed *Primus Circumdedisti Me*. But there is a footnote to this story. Sebastian d'Elcano was *not* actually the first man to circumnavigate the globe. This was a slave who had been captured in the Moluccas – the spice islands north of Australia – and brought to Lisbon. In Lisbon he was bought by Magellan who took him aboard one of his ships before sailing into the sunset in 1519. When the ship reached the spice island of his birth after crossing the Pacific, the slave, Enrique de Molucca, was returning home after a journey which had taken him right round the world.

HERNAN CORTÉS 1485-1547

B orn into a noble family in Spain, Cortés was 11 when Colum-bus first set foot on the American mainland. In 1504, aged 19, he sailed to the Indies to seek his fortune and, while he was there, took part in the conquest of Cuba. By 1517 he was mayor of Santiago – Cuba's then capital – and persuaded the island's gover-nor to give him 11 ships and 600 men with which to sail west to search for gold and 'any other kind of wealth'. What followed was one of the greatest and most terrible stories of conquest in history.

After some skirmishes in and around Yucatán on what is now the Mexican coast – where Cortés gained intelligence from local Indians, among them a woman named Marina (or 'Malinche'), who became his mistress and interpreter – the small force landed at Veracruz just before Easter 1519. They faced the vast armies of Montezuma, the Aztec ruler of an orderly, highly organised civilisation.

At first they were welcomed by the Aztecs as possible reincarnations of the Feathered Serpent god Quetzalcoatl. Emissaries were sent bearing generous gifts, including quantities of gold, which excited the Spaniards' greed. When Cortés received orders to return, he sent one ship back to Spain promising the king lots of gold. He then boldly burnt his boats to prevent desertions and set out for the capital, Tenochtitlán, with just 350 men and a few horses. The Aztecs were terrified of the Spaniards' horses, of their savage mastiffs – which, if provoked, tore their victims apart – and of their iron weapons which sliced through wooden shields.

As they marched inland, Cortés made allies of local chiefs, who resented the Aztec taxes and joined forces with him.

After several battles in which he defeated greatly superior armies and then slaughtered the survivors, he and his men arrived at Tenochtitlán, then the largest city in the Americas. There he was greeted by Montezuma and shown around. What he saw amazed him. There were huge pyramids reeking of blood from the thousands of human sacrifices. There was an enormous and highly efficient canal system with aqueducts bringing in fresh water and floating gardens supplying a market attended by 20,000 people daily. Here you could buy sweet drinks made from honey and sugar cane, chickens, game birds and 'small gelded dogs which they breed for eating' as well as glazed earthenware pitchers and pots, spun cottons and maize, the staple bread. Cortés wrote:

> I will say only that these people live almost like those in
> Spain, and in as much harmony and order as there, and
> considering that they are barbarous and so far from the
> knowledge of God and cut off from all civilized nations
> it is truly remarkable to see what they have achieved in all
> things.

The population of the city was around a quarter of a million.

Cortés: ruthlessly destroyed the ancient Aztec civilisation

Hearing that the garrison he had left behind at Veracruz was mutinying, Cortés went to settle matters himself, after putting a tough soldier, Pedro Alvarado, in charge of the city and imprisoning Montezuma as a hostage. While he was gone, tensions rose between the Spaniards and the Aztec nobility and Alvarado treacherously slaughtered thousands of Aztecs at a festival. Cortés returned to find the city in turmoil and, under mysterious circumstances, Montezuma was killed. The Spaniards escaped from the city and laid siege to it with the help of the Aztecs' enemies, the Tlaxcalans. The siege lasted 93 brutal days, during which many died of starvation and many others were slaughtered. Only 60,000 of the original population survived.

Through ruthless cruelty and helped by guile and a devastating epidemic of smallpox, to which the Aztecs had no resistance, Cortés utterly destroyed the Aztec civilisation, one of the greatest the world has known, and then succeeded in pacifying the whole of their territory. Mexico City was founded on the ruins of the ancient capital and Cortés was appointed governor and captain general of what was, for 300 years, to be called New Spain. Three years later, he was relieved of his post and returned to Spain to face investigations. He lost much of his huge fortune and died on a small estate near Seville in 1547.

FRANCISCO PIZARRO C.1477-1541

Pizarro was the discoverer, conqueror and destroyer of the Inca empire – the last great empire unknown to the rest of humanity. Born, like most of the other *conquistadores*, in Spain's rugged Extremadura, he was a cousin of Cortés, but of very different stock; illegitimate and illiterate, he was to conquer what is now Peru with just 168 men and 62 horses, thus pulling off one of the most spectacular military victories in recorded history.

He first sailed to the New World in 1502 aged about 25, and spent the next 20 years fighting brutal battles against the indigenous inhabitants of various Caribbean islands. In 1513 he was a lieutenant under the Spanish explorer, Vasco Núñez de Balboa, when Balboa crossed the Panama isthmus, sighted the Pacific Ocean for the first time and claimed it for Spain, although it was to be called the South Sea until Magellan reached it 16 years later and named it the Pacific. Ten years later, Pizarro acquired one of the few ships to have been built on the western side of the new continent and, having heard rumours of a rich land to the south, determined he would be the first to reach it.

His voyage was a disaster and he returned to Panama having found nothing. Two years later, his second attempt fared little better, with most of his men mutinying, but he did capture an ocean-going Inca trading raft carrying tempting examples of an advanced civilization: gold and silver ornaments, embroidered cloths, jewels and pottery. He and the few men who stayed with him also landed on the mainland, where they were dazzled by the architecture and stonework of coastal towns – outposts of the Inca empire – and were received hospitably.

Returning to Spain, he received from King Charles I a licence for his proposed expedition and authority over any lands he conquered. Returning to Panama with more men, including family and friends, his third expedition set out at the end of 1530, at first by ship and then overland; it was almost two years before they eventually met the enormous Inca army.

By great good fortune, they arrived in the Inca heartland in the midst of a bloody civil war between the two sons of the last paramount Inca emperor. He had just died of either smallpox or measles, diseases to which indigenous Americans had no immunity and which had raced ahead of the arriving Spaniards. Untold millions were to die from these diseases, making the conquest of most of the Americas much easier and leaving great swathes of country empty of people.

Pizarro and Atahualpa, the victorious brother, met on 16 November 1532 in the town of Cajamarca, where the Spaniards had been comfortably lodged in buildings around the main square. The mighty Inca arrived resplendent in gold and jewels and carried in a litter born by 80 Inca lords, accompanied by a ceremonial parade with thousands of unarmed retainers in elaborate uniforms, chanting as they advanced. Hundreds of Peruvians crowded into the square in their wake.

Francisco Pizarro, painted by Amable-Paul Coutan

To the complete surprise of his host and against seemingly over-whelming odds, Pizarro launched an attack with his few men. They charged at the Peruvians and slaughtered them unmercifully with their razor-sharp swords. Within a couple of hours six or seven thousand Indians lay dead, while Atahualpa was toppled from his litter and captured. As ransom for his release, Pizarro demanded a large room to be filled with gold and silver, and for the next eight months trains of llamas brought the treasure – beautiful artifacts – which Pizarro's men melted down into 15 tons of solid gold and silver. On 26 July 1533 Atahualpa was (wrongly) accused of organising an army for his own rescue, given a summary trial and garrotted.

The still tiny army of Spaniards, now 500 men, due to reinforcements brought in by Hernando de Soto and Francisco de Orellana, was now free to march on the capital, Cusco, where they were welcomed by Atahualpa's rival brother, Huáscar, before ransacking the town and melting down yet more gold and silver treasures. The whole excellent Inca system of governance was destroyed, store houses emptied, herds slaughtered, buildings razed and replaced with churches; with thousands of people dying from disease, the Peruvians became the servants of their Spanish masters.

Seven years later, in 1540, Pizarro sent his youngest brother Gonzalo to take over the Inca's northern capital, Quito, in what is now Ecuador. Tempted by rumours of fabulous wealth to the east, the mythical El Dorado, Gonzalo set off with 220 Spaniards down from the Andean highlands into the Amazon rainforest. His second-in-command and contemporary (both were only 30 years old) was Francisco de Orellana. Things went badly wrong as soon as they arrived in the dense forests, for which they were completely ill-equipped. For ten terrible months they floundered about until, in despair, they built a boat. Orellana, with 50 men, headed downstream to seek supplies. But they were swept on by the flood until there was no chance of returning.

"Pizarro seizing the Inca of Peru" by John Everett Millais

For another eight months they continued down what turned out to be the mightiest river in the world. They endured terrible hunger, met friendly Indians, who helped them, and unfriendly ones, with whom they battled. Many of the latter resembled (and probably were) women, with braided hair. They were fierce and doughty fighters, prompting Orellana to name the river after the legendary race of warrior women in Greek mythology, the Amazons. Incredibly, Orellana, and all but fourteen of his men, survived, managing to reach the sea and then sail round the coast to Venezuela, where they completed, by mistake, one of the greatest feats of exploration of all time.

JAMES COOK 1728-1779

The English naval captain, James Cook, was a brilliant cartographer, or mapmaker, and the most respected of Pacific explorers. He discovered more of the earth's surface than any other person in history. Between 1768 and 1779 he led three major voyages of discovery, becoming the most famous navigator of his day.

Britain's first scientific expedition to the South Seas had two purposes. The first was to observe the Transit of Venus across the sun, a rare astronomical event which, if properly understood, could advance the causes of both science and navigation by helping determine the distance of the earth from the sun. (More specifically, it would also help the Royal Society in London to measure longitude.) The best place to witness the Transit, it was thought, was the newly discovered Pacific island of Tahiti.

Cook's second objective was to go in search of the Great Southern Continent of *Terra Australis*, a fabled land, reputedly of great

Capt: James Cook
of the Endeavour.

*James Cook discovered more of the earth's surface
than anyone else in history. (Portrait by William Hodges)*

wealth. Accompanying Cook in the *Endeavour* were two naturalists, Joseph Banks and Daniel Solander, an astronomer and
two artists. After an idyllic couple of months in Tahiti – where
the people, especially the women, were extraordinarily friendly –
Cook and his crew sailed due south and then west for four months
until the east coast of an unknown country came into view.

This was New Zealand. It had first been seen by Abel Tasman
125 years before, but now Cook spent six months meticulously
charting both the north and south islands, and proving that

49

Plymouth

Tahiti

Rio de Janeiro

Cabo de Hornos

James Cook's first voyage

they were not part of a continent. Sailing west again at last, the *Endeavour* made landfall at Botany Bay on the coast of New Holland (Australia), which Cook named in honour of the collecting fervour of his naturalists, who gathered many unique specimens.

His men became the first Europeans to encounter the local Aborigines, from whom they learnt that the curious jumping creatures they had so often seen were called 'kangurus'. At the same time Cook claimed the entire coastline as British territory, thus transforming the British Empire and opening up a new world for colonisation. One of the most impressive feats of navigation in Pacific history then followed, as he made his way home through deadly reefs and uncharted waters.

On Cook's second ground-breaking voyage, only a year later, he finally put to rest the myth that there was a Southern Continent by sailing the whole way round Antarctica, but without ever setting eyes on it, although his ship crossed the Antarctic Circle, the first ship ever known to do so, and must have been very close to land at times. Now in command of HMS *Resolution*, Cook was to map much of the Pacific Ocean so accurately that copies of his charts were still in use in the mid 20th century. His achievements as a navigator cannot be over-stated but they were not the only reason posterity has cause to be grateful to him, as he also successfully pioneered the use of fruit and sauerkraut to combat scurvy.

Ironically, and unlike many great explorers, he was exceptionally tolerant and kind to the many native peoples he encountered, which made his eventual death at the hands of the Hawaiians all the more tragic. It happened on his third and final voyage in HMS *Discovery*, the purpose of which was to return home a Tahitian who had been brought to England and then to seek the Northwest Passage linking the Atlantic and Pacific oceans and, it was hoped, providing a speedy route between the two.

On his way from Tahiti north, he did not expect to see any more land until he reached the coast of North America. Instead, after less than a month's sailing, he spotted a series of volcanic islands which he named the Sandwich Islands in honour of the then First Lord of the Admiralty, the Earl of Sandwich. Eventually they were renamed and became Hawaii, the 50th state of the United States of America. Within days of making the first landfall, he was describing a now familiar activity in his diary:

> A diversion the most common is upon the water, where there is a very great sea and surf breaking upon the shore. The men sometimes 20 or 30 go without the swell of the surf, and lay themselves flat upon an oval piece of plank about their size and breadth… They wait the time for the greatest swell that sets on shore, and altogether push forward with their arms to keep on its top; it sends them in with a most astonishing velocity.

Cook continued to Vancouver Island and on through the Bering Straits, but was unable to enter the Arctic Ocean due to a wall of ice. Returning to Hawaii he and his men at first received a rapturous welcome, but after a few weeks the mood suddenly changed when one of the *Discovery's* boats was stolen. Cook went ashore with a party of well-armed marines and took a local chief hostage. While leading the chief back to the shore, he was attacked by a large, angry mob, clubbed from behind and killed.

MUNGO PARK 1771-1806

Towards the end of the 18th century, a young Scottish doctor, Mungo Park, made two great expeditions into Africa, both commissioned by the African Association to trace the Niger River. He had always longed to travel, and his opportunity came when his botanist brother-in-law introduced him to Sir Joseph Banks, a naturalist who had sailed with Captain Cook before becoming President of the Royal Society and the inspiration behind the Royal Botanic Gardens at Kew.

Banks and a few friends had co-founded the African Association – or, to give it its long-winded full name, the Association for Promoting the Discovery of the Interior Parts of Africa. The founders were inspired by tales of great riches in the interior of the Dark Continent, but their objective was not to colonise. It was to learn about a land mass still much less known than the Americas, and to seek trading partners there. Timbuktu, in particular, generated

Mungo Park: the slaves "viewed me at first with looks of horror, and repeatedly asked if my countrymen were cannibals".

great excitement as the "African El Dorado", a place where even the slaves were reputed to wear gold.

On his first expedition commissioned by the Association in 1795, Park set out up the Gambia River, alone save for a servant and interpreter. For five months, he lay ill at a slave-trading station, where he taught himself the local language, Mandingo. The slaves "viewed me at first with looks of horror, and repeatedly asked if my countrymen were cannibals" – convinced that, if taken to the coast, they would be eaten rather than put to work.

After leaving the river, Park made mixed progress; some of the people he met welcomed him with open arms and helped him; others were hostile, some believing the tall, pale explorer to be a cat-eyed devil who had been dipped in milk. In Ludamar, on the edge of the Sahara desert, he was taken captive by a Moorish chief and all his goods, except for his pocket compass, which was thought to be white man's magic, were confiscated. He was held for three months and abused physically and verbally for much of the time until finally, on 1 July 1796, he escaped with nothing but a horse and the compass. He battled his way through the jungle to the Niger, becoming the first European to describe the river and report which way it ran, a matter of conjecture for centuries and the object of his expedition.

> I saw with infinite pleasure the great object of my mission, the long-sought-for, majestic Niger, glittering in the morning sun, as broad as the Thames at Westminster, and flowing *slowly to the eastwards*.

Though close to Timbuktu by now, he never reached it, prudently deciding to return home with the information he had already collected. Half starved and riddled with disease, he staggered back to the coast, for some of the way travelling with a column of slaves. Back in Britain, where he was hailed as a hero for answering one of the riddles of African geography, he published his diary, *Travels into the interior of Africa*, which became an instant bestseller and is still in print today.

All Park then wanted to do was to settle down as a GP in Peebles and marry his childhood sweetheart, by whom he had four children over the next eight years. But "the cold and lonely heaths and gloomy hills" of Scotland soon began to pall and he did not need much persuading to accept a government commission to return to the Niger as captain of a 43-strong expedition, with the aim of establishing trading posts and discovering where the river went. Things did not go well. Three-quarters of his men died from disease before even reaching the river. By the time he had built a boat from two canoes and was ready to depart downstream, there were only five Europeans, one local guide and three slaves left. In his last letter home to his wife, he wrote that he intended not to stop or land anywhere until he arrived at the coast, which he hoped to reach in about two months.

He succeeded against tremendous odds in getting three-quarters of the way down the Niger – to the place where it flows out into the Gulf of Guinea. Constantly attacked by hostile locals in fleets of canoes, sometimes as many as 60 at a time, he and his handful of surviving companions were able to fight them off, as they were well armed with muskets and a large quantity of ammunition. They finally came to grief at the Bussa Falls. There the boat became stuck on a rock. The hostile locals gathered on the bank were able to attack with bows and arrows and by throwing spears and all of Park's tiny band except one slave, who lived to tell the tale, were killed or drowned.

RICHARD BURTON 1821-1890 AND JOHN HANNING SPEKE 1827-1864

Burton and Speke, two of the best-known explorers of the 19th century, were very different characters, but their lives were inextricably entwined. The Nile is the world's longest river, 4,160 miles from its source to the sea, almost eight times longer than the entire length of Britain from Land's End to John o'Groats. A hundred and sixty years ago it was still a mystery. Where did all that water come from? Both Burton and Speke were determined to answer that one question.

In the 1850s Great Britain, seeking tighter control over the east coast of Africa and increasingly interested in the exploration of

Burton: fell out with Speke over the true source of the Nile

Central Africa, encouraged the Royal Geographical Society to sponsor an expedition to search for the source. They chose Burton and Speke, two officers in the Indian Army, to lead the journey, and on 16 June 1857 the two men set out from Zanzibar.

Richard Burton was an outstanding orientalist, archaeologist, linguist and anthropologist and a controversial diplomat. He wrote more than 50 books covering an amazing diversity of subjects, and his translation of the Arabian Nights remains the most famous ever published. He spent seven years in India attached to the Bombay native infantry, during which time he learned several

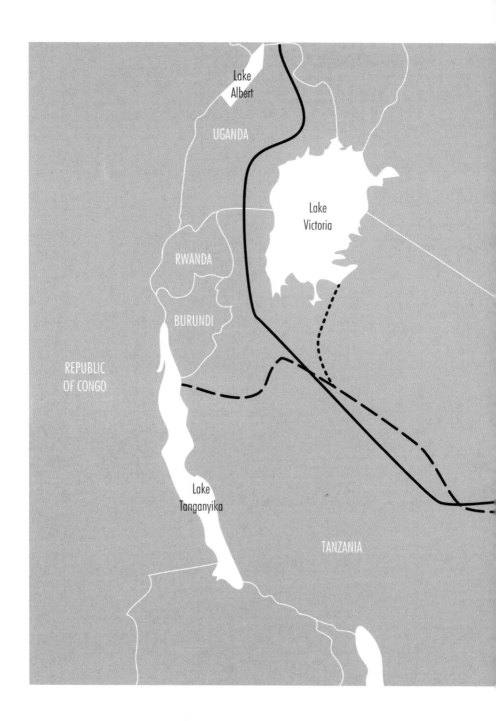

KENYA

Zanzibar

— — Burton and Speke

········ Speke

——— Speke and Grant

The routes taken by Burton and Speke and by Speke and Grant

Indian languages, as well as Arabic, Sanskrit and Pushto.

After visiting Mecca and Medina in disguise in 1853, he prepared an expedition from Berbera on the Somali coast to explore the upper waters of the Nile. Before starting, he went alone disguised as an Arab merchant to visit Harar, the forbidden inland capital, which no European had ever reached. Back on the coast, he and his companions were attacked and wounded by Somalis. One of the men, Lt. Stroyan, was killed, while Burton was speared through both cheeks and Speke received eleven severe spear wounds, two right through his leg. Amazingly, the survivors were able to fight their way to a boat and sail across to Aden.

John Hanning Speke spent ten years serving in India. After being badly wounded with Burton in Africa, he served briefly in the Crimean campaign in Russia before returning to England in 1857 to join the Royal Geographical Society's expedition to explore the Ukerewe, a vast lake rumoured to exist in Central Africa and, if possible to discover the source of the Nile. With 200 porters, as well as an armed escort of 30 men and an Arab guide, the explorers led by Burton and Speke spent 134 gruelling days crossing deserts, marshes and mountains. They suffered from malaria, sickness and exhaustion, and for much of their journey, were carried on litters.

Finally, they reached the eastern shores of Lake Tanganyika, the first Europeans to set eyes on it. For several months they searched the lake in dugout canoes, hoping to find an outlet, but failing to do so. While Burton lay ill, recuperating, Speke took a small party north, found a lake which he named Lake Victoria and proclaimed that he had discovered the source of the Nile.

Burton was furious and refused to believe him, clinging to the false hope that Lake Tanganyika might yet prove to be the true source. For four months the pair struggled acrimoniously back to the coast, and the rift between them only deepened when Speke returned to England ahead of Burton and triumphantly announced his success in the great search.

Speke returned to Africa in 1960 with another explorer, James Grant, to verify his discovery. In the northeast corner of Lake Victoria he found and named the Ripon Falls, which confirmed that the Nile did, indeed flow from there. Back in England, the Royal Geographical Society accepted Speke's claim but others continued to question it, and eventually he was challenged to a debate with his former leader, Richard Burton. The debate was set to take place in Bath in September 1864. Tragically, on the afternoon before it, Speke shot himself while at a partridge shoot on his cousin's estate. Many suspected his death to be suicide, but it seems unlikely that he meant to kill himself as the accident happened while he was clambering over a wall in full view of his cousin and the gamekeeper. Shortly before his own death, Burton finally accepted Speke's discovery and wrote a letter withdrawing every harsh word he had uttered against him.

MERIWETHER LEWIS 1774-1809 & WILLIAM CLARK 1770-1838

When President Thomas Jefferson decided to send an expedition to find a practical route to the Pacific coast, he chose his 29-year-old personal secretary, Meriwether Lewis, to lead it. A Scotsman, Alexander Mackenzie, had already become the first European to cross the continent north of Mexico a dozen years before, travelling mostly by birch-bark canoe on rivers through Canada. This time, however, the plan was for a major scientific mission that would show the world that Americans were capable of state-of-the-art exploration.

There were significant political and economic motives for the trip, too, as the United States had just negotiated what was called the 'Louisiana Purchase' from Napoleon, thus acquiring a vast area of land in the middle of the continent from the French –

Lewis, left, who handled the science, and Clark, who took charge of the men

about half the largely unexplored territory the expedition would be travelling through. At the same time, the Pacific Northwest was being claimed by both the British and the Spanish. It was felt that the US had to move quickly to establish its authority west of the Mississippi.

Although a few fur traders had penetrated the vast plains, rivers and mountains which lay beyond the Mississippi, the geography was little understood and the land was controlled by powerful Indian tribes. Before setting out, Lewis wrote to an old army friend, William Clark, who was four years his senior, offering him co-captaincy of the expedition, with rank and responsibility 'in all respects [to] be precisely such as my own'.

Extraordinarily, this worked and there is no record of any dispute between them. A division of responsibilities was agreed on: Lewis would handle the scientific objectives, often walking on the river bank collecting, examining and measuring everything; Clark would take charge of the men, the maps and the meals. They both kept detailed and extensive journals which together totalled more than one million words and provided a richness of detail without parallel in the history of exploration. Their party consisted of 33 frontiersmen and soldiers, who left St Louis in the spring of 1805. All but one, who died of appendicitis, returned safely 28 months later, having travelled more than 9,000 miles.

After two months dragging their boats up the rapid, snag-infested Missouri for a thousand miles, they entered a landscape unlike any they had seen: the Great Plains. An uninterrupted sea of grass stretched to the distant horizon on every side, populated by immense herds of antelope, elk and buffalo. Here they were in the country of the Sioux nation, equestrians who followed the buffalo herds and lived in skin tipis. When they reached the hills of the Continental Divide, they were in Shoshone Territory and at first received a hostile welcome. But one of their party was a teenage Indian girl, a war captive called Sacagawea, married to a French-Canadian trapper; with them was their six-month-old baby, who had been born on the journey. In a moment of high drama, Sacagawea suddenly recognised the Shoshone chief as her long-lost brother and embraced him emotionally.

This changed the mood completely, and from then on the expedition was guided towards the pass over the Rocky mountains. Their troubles were far from over, however, and for three months they endured a hellish ordeal, struggling through blizzards across steep slopes littered with fallen timber before finally sighting the ocean. 'O! the joy' Clark wrote in his diary. They had hoped to meet a trading ship and so sail home by sea, but none appeared and they spent a miserable winter on the Oregon coast waiting for the snows to melt, so that they could retrace their steps back across the continent. On 23 September 1806 their canoes reached St Louis again and they were greeted deliriously, as they had long been given up for lost.

The failure to achieve their original purpose – finding a route by

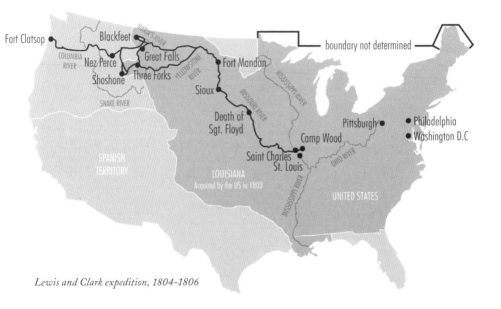

Lewis and Clark expedition, 1804-1806

water through to the Pacific – had exploded the myth of an easy Northwest Passage, as they had demonstrated that a great range of mountains lay in the way. But they had defined the aspirations of a nation about to flourish that it would stretch from east to west, 'from sea to shining sea'.

DAVID LIVINGSTONE 1813-1873

B orn into a devoutly religious and highly literate family in
Blantyre, Scotland, Livingstone worked in a cotton mill from
the age of 10 in order to pay for his education. He put himself
through medical school in Glasgow before moving to London
where he was ordained and trained as a medical missionary. From
then on, apart from two trips back to Britain, he spent all his adult
life in Africa, where he became famous more as an explorer than
as a missionary. He was passionately opposed to the slave trade
and believed that the promotion of legitimate global commerce,
using the rivers of Africa as a vast interlocking communications
network – 'Highways into the interior,' he called them – would
modernise the fragmented continent and so drive out the slavers
whom he saw terrorizing the Africans. His motto was 'Christianity, Commerce and Civilization'.

For the first eight years he was often accompanied by his long-

Livingstone: trained as a medical missionary

suffering wife, Mary, who bore him six children during their arduous travels establishing missions before she returned to Britain and lived in abject penury for four years while Livingstone continued to roam Africa.

When he reached the great Zambezi river, he first explored upstream, heading west, then over the watershed and down to the coast of Angola at Luanda, which he reached after six tough months. The rains set in and his relatively small party (only a few dozen Africans loaned to him by a friendly chief) ran out of goods to trade. By the time he arrived at Luanda Livingstone was very ill with malaria. But he refused to take a ship from there to Britain and instead, after four months spent recuperating, started back across Africa to make one of the great epic journeys of all time – the first crossing of the continent from west to east.

It took him two years, one to retrace his steps, the second to follow the Zambezi downstream to the Indian Ocean. His first discovery was Africa's largest waterfall, well known already, of course, to the local inhabitants, who called it Mosi-ao-Tunya, 'The Smoke that Thunders'. Livingstone promptly renamed it the Victoria Falls after his Queen. From Quelimane near the mouth of the Zambezi, he sailed back to Southampton to be greeted by Mary and discover that he had become extremely famous through the publication of his letters home. He had been awarded the Founder's Medal of the Royal Geographical Society the year before and was shortly to be made a Fellow of the Royal Society, as well as receiving several honorary degrees. At breakneck speed, he wrote his book *Missionary Travels and Researches in South Africa*, which became one of the biggest best-sellers of the century. He gave a series of well-attended public lectures, had an audience with Queen Victoria and was sponsored by the British government to undertake another expedition.

This expedition, back to the Zambezi, left England in March 1858 with Livingstone as the leader, accompanied by his wife, his brother Charles and the great expedition artist, Thomas Baines. Mary was pregnant again and so she stayed in Cape Town before leaving for the interior to join her parents, who were also missionaries. Her husband's expedition, which lasted six years, was a disaster. Navigation on the Zambezi proved impossible because of the treacherous Quebrabasa cataracts, which Livingstone had failed to find on his previous journey. He was a hopelessly inept leader and fell out with most of the Europeans.

Mary rejoined him after four years, but died of malaria soon afterwards. Livingstone was depressed and angry when the expedition was eventually recalled to London because of its increasing costs and the failure to find a navigable route to the interior. But at least the scientists who took part managed to contribute large collections of botanical, ecological, geological, and ethnographic material to scientific institutions; and the expedition had reached – and put a boat on – Lake Malawi, which Livingstone called Lake Nyasa.

On his return, Livingstone experienced great difficulty in raising funds for further exploration, as his reputation was at a low ebb. His last expedition in 1866 included no other Europeans, its purpose being to confirm the source of the Nile. Once again things went wrong, this time due to illness and violent encounters with slave traders, and Livingstone vanished from sight. He was famously found living reluctantly on Arab help in Ujiji, by Henry Morton Stanley in November 1871, and greeted with 'Dr Livingstone, I presume'. The two men explored Lake Tanganyika together before Stanley left. Increasingly ill and having to be carried on a litter, Livingstone continued feverishly to search unsuccessfully for the source of the Nile until he died a year later. His faithful African servants embalmed his body and, amazingly, succeeded in bringing him back to England, where he was buried in Westminster Abbey.

HENRY MORTON STANLEY 1841-1904

He was born John Rowlands, out of wedlock, in Wales and spent his childhood in a workhouse. He joined the crew of a ship sailing to New Orleans when he was 18, and changed his name to Henry Stanley after a prominent local cotton broker. He added Morton later. For a wild decade he fought in the Confederate army in the American Civil War, was captured and conscripted into the Union army and then the navy, from both of which he deserted before becoming a reporter and covering, among other stories, the suppression of Native Americans in the west.

The owner and editor of the New York Herald, James Gordon Bennett, sent him to cover the British invasion of Abyssinia in 1867, which made his name and led to his being chosen to return to Africa and find David Livingstone, who had been missing for almost two years. The story of their meeting has become the stuff of legends, culminating in the famous words: "Dr Livingstone, I presume?"

'Dr Livingstone, I presume?'

The two men travelled together for a while, exploring the region and proving that there was no connection between Lake Tanganyika and the Nile before Stanley returned to announce his coup to the world. Livingstone was not to see another white face before his death a year later.

Stanley had been inspired by his meeting with Livingstone and he returned to Africa several times. First, he established, by becoming the first person to circumnavigate it, that Lake Victoria, the second largest freshwater lake in the world, had only a single outlet and thus he validated Speke's contention that it was the source of the Nile. He then mounted a major expedition to follow the Congo river to its mouth in the Atlantic. The three European officers and most of the 300 porters he set off with perished on the

7,000-mile journey, which lasted 999 days and involved 32 battles with hostile locals, But Stanley had achieved the first crossing of the African continent and went on to become involved with King Leopold II of Belgium in establishing the colony of the Belgian Congo.

His last African adventure was as leader of an expedition to rescue Emin Pasha (Eduard Schnitzer), an Ottoman-German Jewish doctor and naturalist who was trapped with a small army in the south of Sudan by the forces of the Mahdi, who had earlier taken the life of General Gordon at Khartoum, just before he could be rescued. Emin Pasha, appointed to govern the province of Equatoria as Gordon's successor, managed to get messages out via Zanzibar, which led the British public to believe that he, too, was in mortal danger from the Mahdists and needed rescuing. This generated great interest in mounting a relief expedition and £32,000 was raised, the equivalent of almost £3 million today. But the true story was much more complicated and, in the end, it turned out, Emin did not need or want to be "rescued" and actually saved the exhausted rescuers when they eventually reached him.

Stanley chose an extraordinarily difficult route, going up the Congo and then through the Ituri forest, which he was the first to describe. The trees were so dense that light could barely penetrate them, giving Stanley the title of his subsequent book, *In Darkest Africa*. Many of his men died of hunger, others after being shot with poisoned arrows by the indigenous pygmies.

Once again two-thirds of the expedition died, and the behaviour of some of Stanley's fellow Europeans damaged his reputation. One, James Sligo Jameson, heir to the Irish whisky manufacturer, Jameson's, bought an 11-year-old girl and offered her to cannibals so he could document and sketch how she was cooked and eaten. Stanley is, however, credited with putting Mount Ruwenzori on the map during the return journey, and thereby locating the fabled Mountains of the Moon. Emin Pasha stayed in Africa and eventually took service with the Germans, who were beginning to colonise the east coast.

Today, Stanley's name evokes contrasting responses. Some see him as a heroic explorer who exhibited great courage in the face of dangers that should have cost him his life on many occasions. Others see him, because of his connection with the ruthless colonialist, King Leopold II of Belgium, as representing the worst of 19th century European penetration of Africa.

NAIN SINGH C.1830-1882

The portentously named Great Trigonometric Survey of India was launched by the British government in the 1860s. One of the most ambitious exploration projects of the 19th century, its purpose was to map a huge area not just of India but of Central Asia. Alarm bells were ringing in London about Russia, which was trying to expand its influence into Asia and which, the British feared, might even seek to conquer India. Knowing in detail the geography of the region was thus of vital importance in what was known as the 'Great Game'.

There was a major problem, however. In some of the regions beyond India, such as Tibet, westerners were unwelcome – and banned from entry. Thomas Montgomerie, a captain of the British survey team, solved the problem by training native Indian surveyors, who would be able to travel with less risk and could disguise themselves as traders or lamas (holy men). Between 1865 and 1875, these native surveyors, known as Pundits, marched thousands of miles through the Himalayas, always in great danger, mapping vast areas forbidden to Europeans.

Nain Singh was the first and perhaps the greatest of the pundits. He took precise footpaces of thirty-three inches exactly, used a Buddhist rosary to keep exact count of the paces in a day, or between two landmarks, and used a prayer wheel fitted to hide his notes and conceal a compass. The territory he covered was almost entirely unmapped.

Nain Singh was from the Himalayan region of Tibet, a schoolmaster in Kumaon who spoke Hindi, Persian, English and Tibetan. After a rigorous training course at the Survey's headquarters at Dehra Dun, in northern India, where he learnt to use the sextant to determine latitudes, the compass for taking bearings, the basics of astronomy for night navigation and the use of a thermometer for measuring altitude, he was ready to begin the first secret exploration of Tibet. His code name was No.1. Going north to Katmandu, he attempted to enter Tibet from Nepal.

It was midwinter and the journey took three months as he struggled over snowbound passes, surviving a series of narrow escapes from Chinese border guards. On reaching Lhasa, he stayed for another three months during which he calculated the latitude and altitude of the city, both unknown at the time, with amazing accuracy. Turning westwards, he joined a caravan travelling to Tibet's holy Lake Mansarowar before eventually returning to Dehra Dun. He had 2.5 million paces on his rosary, or 1,500 miles. He had also fixed the course off the Brahmaputra from its source near Mansarowar to Lhasa, and determined the height of 33 previously uncharted peaks and passes.

On his journey, he had heard intriguing tales of gold mines in a remote area and so, six months later, he was sent off again, this time with two other Pundits. They came back with a mass of valuable information, having between them surveyed some 18,000 miles and 80 more summits.

Later expeditions confirmed Singh as the most celebrated of all the Pundits. After eight years of travel, aged nearly 50, he was sent on a mission to Yarkand, north of the Himalayas in the Chinese desert of Takla Makan. On his return he was awarded the Patron's Medal of the Royal Geographical Society for being 'the man who has added a greater amount of positive knowledge to the map of Asia than any individual of our time'. The president of the RGS, Sir Clements Markham, who became Secretary of State for India, said:

> The journey performed between July 1874 and March 1875 by the Pundit Nain Singh, of the Great Trigonometrical Department, is the most important, as regards geographical discovery, that has been made by any native explorer.

There were other Pundits who carried out marathon and courageous surveys in India. Kishen Singh, for example – code-named 'A.K.' – covered 3,000 miles to reach the Chinese Mongolian frontier, returning after four years and 5.5 million paces, ragged and emaciated, but with his maps and secret surveying instruments intact, having been all but written off at Dehra Dun. Some Pundits were sent back, and others were tortured and executed, but collectively their achievement was astonishing: despite the risks, they were the first to map the Himalayas.

FRANCIS GARNIER 1839-1873

The Frenchman Francis Garnier belongs among the giants of exploration, even though he was actually a very small man. Like David Livingstone, who was driven by a hatred of the slave trade, Garnier had an obsession: in his case it was to expand the French empire at a time when it was declining. Bizarrely, both men were to share an award at the first International Congress in 1871 and both men received the Gold Medals from the Royal Geographical Society, in 1855 and 1870 respectively.

At a time when France was seeking an overseas empire, the acquisition of Indo-China looked like a solution, and the Mekong River offered a potential 'highway of commerce', a backdoor waterway into China. A Mekong Exploration Commission was formed. Because Garnier was too young, being only 27, the leadership was given to Doudart de Lagrée, another Frenchman 20 years his senior, who knew Cambodia well, but who had never been into the interior and who fell ill and died en route. So Garnier, the inspiring spirit of the expedition, soon found himself in command after all.

In June 1866 two small paddle-driven gunboats with six French officers and a 16-man escort set off from Saigon (today's Ho Chi Minh City). They reached the site of the ancient Khmer capital at Angkor, which was then under Thai rule, surveyed it and claimed it for Cambodia, and so for France.

They then failed completely to ascend the many rapids between Cambodia and Laos in their gunboats, which had to be abandoned. The expedition continued in long, local pirogues (long canoes made from single tree trunks); these were laboriously paddled and poled through the rough water. All six Frenchmen suffered badly from malaria and Garnier slipped into a coma, thereby missing the sensational Khon Falls, which are bigger than the Victoria and Niagara Falls combined and around which the pirogues were pulled. As a result, he always mistakenly believed the Mekong to be potentially navigable and so thought that it would make a viable route for French trade into China.

For well over a year Garnier and his men struggled up the unexplored and increasingly difficult Mekong until they reached the Burmese border and the Shan States. There they finally abandoned their boats and made their way across a sodden wilderness hindered by heavy monsoon rains into China at Kunming, where Lagrée died and Garnier formally took charge. From there they reached the upper Yangtze, down which they sailed. On 6 June 1868, two years to the day since they had left Saigon, the expedition surprised the world by presenting itself at the French consulate in the Yangtze port of Hankou. They had successfully accomplished one of the greatest expeditions of the 19th century.

Although feted in London, Garnier's achievement was not recognised in France. He sailed back east in disgust and was discredited when killed during a mad-cap bid to capture Hanoi and

Garnier: driven by an obsession to expand the French empire

claim its Red River as another way into China. While driving off some bandits, who had attacked him and his men outside the west gate of Hanoi, he slipped and fell into a ditch. Surrounded, he fired off the six rounds from his revolver, but was pierced with sabres and lances; his head was cut off and his body horribly mutilated before the bandits ran away. His bloodied corpse was recovered and carried back to the city.

Not until the 1880s did France act on his recommendations and challenge the British in Southeast Asia by creating French Indo-China. This empire consisted of Vietnam, Cambodia and Laos, all linked by the hopelessly unnavigable Mekong.

GERTRUDE BELL 1868-1926

Gertrude Bell was an Arabist, explorer, mountaineer, archaeologist, writer, poet, intelligence expert and, as if this was
not enough to occupy a life tragically cut short at 57, co-founder of
the modern state of Iraq.

Born into a very wealthy family, she was the first woman to
achieve a First in Modern History at Oxford, the first woman
to be awarded a prize by the Royal Geographical Society, and
the first woman officer in British military intelligence. She also
became the first person to climb one of the most prominent peaks
in the Alps.

At 32 she made her debut in the desert, a camel trek across Syria.
On her landmark Arabian expedition of 1913-14 she struck out
alone from Damascus to the stronghold of Hail in the Nafud
Desert of what is today Saudi Arabia. She had already shown
herself to be intrepid, but this was to be a formidable journey,

undertaken in part to escape the turmoil of her relationship with a married army officer, Charles Doughty-Wylie, later recipient of a posthumous Victoria Cross for gallantry at Gallipoli. It was a dangerous expedition through tortuous sand dunes to somewhere unseen by European eyes for 20 years and she was put under house arrest on arrival. Writing about it in one of her many letters, she captures the spirit of the desert well:

> I have known loneliness in solitude now, for the first time, and in the long days of camel riding and the long evenings of winter camping, my thoughts have gone wandering from the camp fire… Then comes the dawn, soft and beneficent, stealing over the wide plain and down the long slopes of the little hollows, and in the end it steals into my dark heart also…

She returned with copious information on the tribes of the area, as well as acute insights into relations between the Rashids and Sauds, rivals for power in the Arabian peninsula. Along with the mapping and surveying she had carried out, this intelligence was of the greatest value for London, which was also seeking information on routes for the advance of the British Army into Palestine.

Two years later she was appointed Oriental Secretary to the administrator in Baghdad and she threw herself into Middle Eastern politics with gusto. Her wide-ranging intellect, linguistic talent and unconquerable will, together with resolute courage amid hair-raising adventures in a foreign world even more male-dominated than her own in Britain, made her an outstanding and significant figure – it often made her unpopular too. Sir Mark Sykes, one half of the Anglo-French team which in 1916 drew the infamous Sykes-Picot line carving up the region between the two colonial powers, found her particularly maddening. But her opposition to their plan was well founded: history has revealed

Bell revelled in her role at the heart of Middle East decision-making

what a mistake the Sykes-Picot line was and it remains a problem to this day.

Meanwhile, Gertrude Bell revelled in her role at the heart of the decision-making about Iraq's borders, borders which would encompass Kurds, and Sunni and Shia Arabs. A gratifying procession of ambitious sheiks swept through her office and house. "These are the people I love", she wrote, "I know every tribal chief of any importance throughout the whole length and breadth of Iraq." It was true; she did; but when King Faisal was installed on the throne she had outlived her usefulness. She founded the National Museum and became Iraq's Director of Antiquities, but it was not enough for her and on the night of 11 July 1926 she took an overdose of sleeping pills.

In 1980, as the Royal Geographical Society celebrated its 150th

"I know every tribal chief throughout the whole length and breadth of Iraq."

anniversary, there were plans to honour Gertrude Bell in a commemorative set of postage stamps featuring great British explorers. One can only imagine her reaction if she had learned of the Foreign Office's response: it vetoed the proposal for fear of offending Saddam Hussein.

ALEXANDER VON HUMBOLDT 1769 – 1859

Described by Charles Darwin as the greatest scientific traveller who ever lived, Humboldt can also fairly be called the founder of the modern science of ecology. Although his major travels in the Americas only lasted five years, he and his companion, the French botanist Aimé Bonpland, collected a quite astonishing number of specimens (more than 60,000), as well as making ground-breaking observations of things zoological, geological, astronomical and cultural. It took Humboldt the next 30 years and multiple volumes to distil and publish the results.

Born in Prussia, he was a brilliant student and his early studies prepared him well for a life of scientific exploration. In 1796 his mother died leaving him a fortune which he devoted over the rest of his life to research and writing. By this time, now 27, he had already published several learned papers and made valuable contacts throughout European academic society.

After some adventurous travels in Europe, he persuaded the king of Spain to grant him and Bonpland permits to make an expedition to South America. They sailed first to Venezuela in 1800 and set to work at once. Humboldt was fascinated by everything and recorded all his findings and thoughts meticulously. The pair had all sorts of of scientific instruments with them: barometers, chronometers, hygrometers, electrometers, telescopes, sextants, theodolites, quadrants, a dipping needle, compasses, a magnetometer, a pendulum, eudiometers to measure the blueness of the sky, and chemical reagents for analysis. Everything was carted on oxen and mules across the dusty plains of Venezuela and over the towering Andes of Colombia and Ecuador, and by boat along only barely navigable rivers or on extended voyages by sea. Everything that could possibly be measured was measured.

One of the first experiments Humboldt made was into animal electricity, which had long fascinated him. Electric eels were captured by driving horses into their pools, where they discharged their voltage and could be handled. Nonetheless, the explorers had many 'dreadful shocks' while experimenting on and dissecting them.

They travelled right up the Orinoco River and established the existence of a river, the Casiquiare, which links the river basins of the Orinoco with the Amazon. Humboldt documented the lives of several local tribes of American Indians, with whom he developed a close affinity, although he inaccurately described them as cannibals. In Ecuador he and Bonpland climbed several volcanoes, including Chimborazo, then thought to be the highest mountain in the world. They failed to reach the summit, but for the next 30 years Humboldt held the record as the man who had climbed higher than anyone else, having reached 19,286ft. (5878m.)

From local farmers he learned about the rich fertilising proper-

A portrait of Humboldt by Friedrich Georg Weitsch. Charles Darwin called him the greatest scientific traveller who ever lived.

ties of guano and it was Humboldt who brought this discovery back to Europe. The ocean current that flows up the western coast of South America is named after him, as it was his measurements of the sea temperature off the coast of Peru that revealed its existence.

After nearly four years in South America, the two men and their entourage sailed to Mexico where they spent a year travelling to volcanoes, studying Aztec culture and visiting mines. In the US, Humboldt met the president, Thomas Jefferson, and spent a week with him discussing, among other things, the Lewis and Clark expedition, which was due to set off less than a year later.

One of the most remarkable outcomes of the journeys by Humboldt and Bonpland is the huge scientific output they published on their return. In his botanical journal, Bonpland described 4,000 species, but it was Humboldt's many volumes on plants, animals, geology and the indigenous tribes of the Americas which formed the basis for modern plant geography and ecology. In his final massive work, *Kosmos*, he attempted to bring together and record everything then known about science and nature and the connections between them. Over 25 years he published the first four volumes, but died half-way through the fifth, just short of his 90th birthday. He was the last explorer who could consider undertaking such a task – 'a physical description of the universe' – in one book.

ALFRED RUSSEL WALLACE 1823-1913

Wallace, the son of an unsuccessful businessman, grew up in modest circumstances, first in rural Wales, then in Hertford, where he went to the local grammar school. Apart from this, he was entirely self taught – remarkable given that he became one of the 19th century's most distinguished intellectuals. The eighth of nine children, he served as an apprentice at a surveying business run by one of his older brothers, then, briefly, worked as a teacher, but meanwhile devoted as much time as he could to pursuing his interest in natural history, and reading voraciously.

On his first expedition, to South America in 1848, he travelled with his great friend, Henry Walter Bates, who had first introduced him to the delights of beetle-hunting. Later, the two men met up with the botanist, Richard Spruce, so that, for a while, three of the greatest naturalists of the era were collecting along a 50-mile stretch of the Amazon. Wallace continued on his own far up a tributary, the Rio Negro, and spent time with Amerindian tribes, recording their customs, dances and languages, while gathering specimens of monkeys and parrots.

Unfortunately much of the work was in vain. On his return trip to Britain, the ship in which he was sailing caught fire. In the scramble to take to the lifeboats, Wallace was able to grab some of his sketches of fish and palms, but after that could only watch helplessly as most of his belongings burned with the ship, including his collection of animals and birds and almost all of the portfolio of drawings and journals covering the entire three years he had been in South America.

Undeterred, he determined to put together another expedition, and two years later sailed for the Far East. First in and around Singapore, then in Borneo, he settled down to serious collecting, at which he was strikingly adept. He records that on his single most productive day he captured no less than 76 different species of insects and beetles, of which 34 were new to him and so, presumably, to science. During this time, he was taken under the wing of Sir James Brooke, a British soldier and adventurer who founded the kingdom of Sarawak in Borneo and ruled it, as the first White Rajah, from 1841 until his death in 1868. Wallace, in gratitude, named one of his first discoveries after Brooke, a butterfly of exceptional beauty which he called the Rajah Brooke Birdwing.

Moving further east, he reached Bali and then Lombok, where he noted that the bird population was entirely different on the two islands, even though they were only some 20 miles apart. It was his first clue to a notional line which he identified between Borneo and Sulawesi, a line which divides the fauna of Asia from that of Australasia, caused by the way in which, millions of years ago, continental drift separated the two land masses. The line is now known as 'Wallace's line'.

In the Celebes (Sulawesi) and throughout the Moluccas he continued to collect indefatigably, his mind teeming with the incredible diversity of species that he came across. One day, on the island of Gilolo (Halmahera) he began to shiver from a severe bout of malarial fever, but this only spurred him to think even harder about the origins of man and how species change. Suddenly the answer came to him: in every generation the inferior would inevitably be killed off and the superior would remain – that is, 'the fittest would survive'. Back in Ternate, he made a fair copy of his paper and sent it to Charles Darwin, with whom he was already in correspondence, seeking his opinion. Then he prepared for another major voyage, to New Guinea.

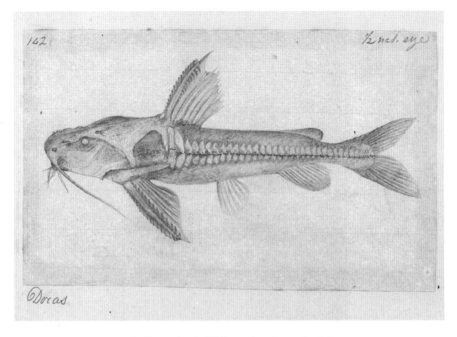

An illustration, by Wallace, of an Amazonian fish

When he returned, there was news of his paper's reception. It had been read, with accompanying texts, by Darwin, at the Linnean Society's meeting of July 1st, 1858. The theory of evolution by natural selection was in the public domain and Darwin himself then went on to publish his *On the Origin of Species.* The two men continued to be friends, greatly admiring one another, and Wallace's role and reputation as a scientific thinker was universally recognised.

HEINRICH BARTH 1821-1865

A highly accomplished scholar and linguist, the German Heinrich Barth stands out as the greatest and most meticulous of desert explorers. For five years between 1850 and 1855 he explored most of the Sahara, travelling vast distances by camel; his anthropological research into the African tribes he encountered is still widely regarded as definitive.

Educated in Berlin, he studied several leading intellectuals, among them Alexander von Humboldt, before joining a major expedition – the grandly titled Central African Expedition, led by the British anti-slavery campaigner James Richardson. Richardson, however, died early on, after crossing the Sahara, and Barth carried on alone. He travelled light, carrying only his compass, his watch and two pistols – completely self-reliant and, as he always would be, happiest on his own.

Already able to speak French, Spanish, Italian, English and

Arabic, he became fluent in five African languages and compiled word lists of another 40. He surveyed the country around Lake Chad, establishing which way the various rivers flowed, crossing the Niger on its way south to the Gulf of Guinea and making his way to Timbuktu. There he was in extreme danger as both a foreigner and a Christian. He assumed the disguise of a travelling Muslim, calling himself Abd el Kerim ('Servant of the Merciful') and struck up a friendship with a renowned spiritual leader, which almost certainly saved his life.

Though short of money and often ill, he carried on regardless, completing comprehensive accounts of the geography, history and ethnography of each country he visited, and with the help of his extraordinary language skills interrogating everyone he met along the way – his servants, passers-by, pilgrims, travelling scholars, local officials and desert nomads.

In all, in this one journey, he covered a breathtaking 10,000 miles overland and his five-volume *Travels and Discoveries in North and Central Africa* remains a classic to this day. The British government had long given him up for dead when he ran into Eduard Vogel, the leader of a mission to find him or discover his fate. By now he was ready to come home and so once more made the long and arduous journey back across the Sahara to Tripoli. He was applauded on his return to London, given an award by the Royal Geographical Society and made a Companion of the Order of Bath, but his outstanding achievements were to be eclipsed by the search for the source of the Nile and the discoveries of Livingstone and Burton. He became increasingly introspective and died aged only 44, a disappointed man. Before he died he wrote that he longed only for

> a night camp in the desert, that immeasurable open space, without ambition and without cares for the thousand little things that torture men here; and for the utter enjoyment

Heinrich Barth: always happiest on his own

Timbuktu seen from a distance by Barth's party, September 7th, 1853. Drawn by Martin Bernatz after a sketch by Barth.

of the freedom that comes at the end of a day's march, stretched out on my mat, with my belongings, my camels and my horse around me.

ROALD AMUNDSEN 1872-1928

In the annals of those who have explored both the Arctic and the Antarctic, Roald Amundsen's achievements are unequalled. He was the first to travel the fabled Northwest Passage by ship, the first to reach the South Pole, and quite probably the first to set eyes – albeit from the air – on the North Pole as well.

Born into a family of Norwegian ship-owners, he always wanted to go to sea, His first major voyage, however, was much longer than he'd anticipated. Joining a Belgian expedition to Antarctica in 1897, as first mate, he inadvertently found himself wintering there with the rest of the crew when their ship became locked in sea ice; they learnt an invaluable lesson: how to survive on fresh seal and penguin meat, and so avoid scurvy.

Three years later, Amundsen managed to scrape together sufficient funds to buy a small fishing trawler with shallow draft, the *Gjoa*. Accompanied by just six men, and narrowly escaping debt collectors who had been chasing him for unpaid bills, he left Trömso in Norway on 16 June 1903 in an attempt to sail through the tangle of frozen islands north of Canada and so traverse between the Atlantic and Pacific oceans. In marked contrast to previous, largely British, expeditions, he hugged the treacherous coasts in his little craft and studied the ways of the Inuit, who taught him and his companions survival skills, such as the use of sled dogs and how to wear animal skins. These were greatly superior to the heavy, woollen parkas, which could not keep, out the cold when wet.

After successfully reaching Alaska, he returned to Norway almost three and a half years later and soon began preparing for an expedition to the North Pole. But when he heard that two Americans – Frederick Cook and Robert Peary – were both claiming to have reached it, he changed his plan, informing his crew well after they had set sail in Nansen's ship, *Fram* (which the other great Norwegian explorer had generously lent him) that the South Pole would be their goal. The rest of the world was kept in ignorance of the change, but he did send a telegram to Captain Scott – who had already set out with the same objective – thus initiating an epic race.

His first attempt in September 1911 had to be abandoned due to extreme weather. On 19 October, with four sledges, four companions and 52 well-chosen dogs, he set out again, taking just under two months to reach the South Pole. He butchered most of his dogs to feed the others. By the time he reached the Pole he had 16 dogs left; only 11 of these made it back to the coast. He had arrived 33 days before Scott's team, who were to find a tent and letter he had left for them there.

With two of his South Pole companions, he spent 1918 and 1925 navigating through the Northeast Passage along the coast of Siberia collecting scientific data and attempting to drift north to the Pole. This passage had already been pioneered in 1878 by the

Amundsen: probably the first man to reach both the North and South Poles

Amundsen with his crew: he left a letter for Captain Scott at the South Pole

Finnish-Swedish explorer Adolf Erik Nordenskiold.

Amundsen, who had obtained Norway's first pilot's licence, then turned to aviation as a way of reaching the North Pole. First, using two specially modified Dornier seaplanes, he made it to 88 degrees north, the northernmost latitude reached by any aircraft up to that time, before landing on the ice and damaging one of the aircraft beyond repair. The other plane was damaged too and took several weeks to fix before he could take off again. Meanwhile, back in Norway, he and his party had been given up for dead.

Amundsen's final expedition was in an airship designed and piloted by the Italian Umberto Nobile. On board were 15 other men, mostly Italian air crew, but also Oscar Wisting, who had accompanied Amundsen to the South Pole. Taking off from Spitsbergen on 11 May 1926, they enjoyed a remarkably smooth and uneventful flight to the Pole, before continuing across the polar icecap to Alaska in a flight which lasted just over 70 hours. Three men had claimed to reach the Pole before Amundsen did: Frederick Cook in 1908, Robert Peary a year later, and Richard Byrd in 1926. Their claims have all been disputed, the evidence suggesting that Amundsen and Oscar Wisting were the first men to *both* poles, one by ground, the other by air.

Two years later, Nobile crashed another airship during a second polar voyage. Amundsen immediately took off in a French flying boat to look for him, despite poor visibility. Presumed to have crashed somewhere in the icy waters of the Barents Sea, his plane has never been found. Nobile survived.

ROBERT FALCON SCOTT
1868-1912

Scott, a Royal Navy captain, rose to fame when he led the mainly scientific Discovery Expedition over the Ross Sea ice shelf in Antarctica in 1902. He set a new southern record by reaching latitude 82 degrees south and returned to England a popular hero. One of his companions was Ernest Shackleton who, four years later, pushed further south towards the Pole, only turning back because of dwindling supplies just 97 miles short of his goal. Reading on a news hoarding of Shackleton's narrow failure, Scott is said to have announced: "I think we had better have a shot next."

The Terra Nova Expedition, as it came to be known, was commanded by Scott. The *Terra Nova*, an old converted whaler, nearly sank on the way out and was then stuck for a long time in the ice,

Scott writing his diary in the Antarctic

causing what turned out to be a fateful delay. Scott was determined to make this, his second expedition, as much about science as about being first to the Pole. Among his important discoveries, from the plant fossils he collected, was proof that Antarctica had once been forested and joined to other continents.

His party included the most accomplished scientists he could find, but their presence slowed him down, adding to his delays. He knew he would have to race the weather; what he didn't know, at first, was that he had a human competitor. The Norwegian Amundsen had a tight-knit group consisting of the world's best dog sledgers and skiers, as well as his 52 racing huskies. Scott had a support team of 65 men which included not just many scientists but their cumbersome instruments.

*The converted whalter, Terra Nova,
making its way through pack ice*

Moreover, while he knew that dogs could drag loads further than men, he was conscious of the suffering they had to endure in sub-zero temperatures, and so planned to use them only at the start. Instead he had brought ponies from Siberia, which turned out to be of poor quality, and innovative motor sledges which soon broke down due to mechanical failures in the cold.

Scott set out 12 days after Amundsen, on 1 November 1910. He still had 360 miles to cover when his rival reached the Pole. By the end of December, the British team of five men, with and without skis, were averaging 13 miles a day while the Norwegians, with their dogs, were averaging 15 miles a day. Only when they reached the immediate vicinity of the Pole did they spot the Norwegians' tracks and realise they had been beaten. Scott wrote in his diary:

> Great God! This is an awful place and terrible enough for
> us to have laboured to it without the reward of priority.

On their dispirited return from the Pole, Scott's men hauled their heavy sledges almost as fast as the Norwegians hauled theirs, but they ran into terrible weather, which slowed them up. Edgar Evans died of hypothermia on the way down a glacier; Titus Oates purposefully left the tent in a blizzard rather than continue to hold back the others. Before he went, he famously said: "I am just going outside and may be some time." Scott, with his two surviving colleagues, Henry Bowers and the doctor, Edward Wilson, almost made it back to their base but failed because of freak weather – one of the coldest spells ever recorded – which also prevented a prearranged support team from reaching them. They died in their final camp only 11 miles short of their supply dump.

Their bodies were recovered eight months later. Among the last things Scott wrote as he lay dying was a letter to his wife, Kathleen. In it, he scribbled: "Make the boy [their son Peter] interested in natural history if you can; it is better than games;

they encourage it at some schools." Peter Scott was to found the World Wildlife Fund and to become perhaps the greatest inspirer of conservation of the 20th century.

we shall stick it out to the end but we are getting weaker of course and the end cannot be far.

It seems a pity, but I do not think I can write more —

R Scott

Last Entry —

For Gods Sake look after our people

The final page of Scott's diary, written shortly before he died

WALLY HERBERT 1934-2007

The son of an English army officer, Wally Herbert was the greatest modern polar explorer. He travelled over 23,000 miles by dog-sled in both the Arctic and Antarctic before making the epic first surface crossing of the Arctic Ocean.

In 1909 an American, Robert Peary, had claimed to be the first man to reach the North Pole, and for sixty years his achievement was generally accepted. More recently, however, close examination of his personal log-book and accompanying evidence have revealed a navigational record that is seriously compromised both by its extraordinary lack of rigour and by the enormity of the distances claimed. At one stage, Peary claimed that when near the Pole he had covered an average of 56 miles a day, suggesting that he travelled at a speed no one had come close to before and no one has managed since.

In 1968, Herbert, with three team-mates, Alan Gill, Ken

Herbert: the greatest modern polar explorer

Hedges and Roy 'Fritz' Koerner, left Point Barrow, Alaska on the longest polar trek in history. Each had a team of husky dogs and they made good progress for the first month or so. A medical crisis stopped them in their tracks 240 miles short of the spot they had picked to spend the winter. Gill, immobilised, probably with a slipped disc, could walk no further, so they were forced to spend five months out of sight of the sun in temperatures routinely below − 30C. (Herbert felt he should be given the chance to recover, refusing pleas from London to have him sent home.) At one point, they were forced to move their entire camp from the slab of floating ice, or ice pan, on which it was based, because the pan had begun to break up. The move had to be made in total darkness.

Not until the winter ended, and they began to see sunlight again, were they able to resume their journey. On 6 April 1969, 60 years to the day after Peary had claimed it to be his, they finally reached the Pole. Herbert described the moment of his arrival thus:

It had been an elusive spot to find and to fix – the North Pole, where two separate sets of meridians meet and all directions are south. Trying to set foot upon it had been like trying to step on the shadow of a bird that was hovering overhead, for the surface across which we were moving was itself a moving surface on a planet that was spinning about an axis beneath our feet.

On 29 May 1969, Herbert and his team completed the 16-month crossing of the Arctic when they reached land on Little Blackboard Island, northeast of Spitsbergen. If Peary's navigation was indeed at fault, they were the first to reach the Pole over the ice.

Almost 20 years later, Herbert was commissioned by the National Geographic Society, which had supported Peary's claim, to write an assessment of Peary's 1909 diary and astronomical observations. These had not been made accessible to researchers for several decades. As Herbert researched this material, he concluded that the explorer must have falsified his records and had not reached the Pole. His book, *The Noose of Laurels: The Race to the North Pole* (1989), caused a furore when it was published. But his evaluation of Peary's records and conclusion has now been widely accepted.

Only three weeks after Herbert and his team reached Spitzbergen, Neil Armstrong became the first person to land on another planet and suddenly terrestrial exploration seemed tame by comparison. As a result, Wally Herbert's extraordinary achievement did not receive the full recognition it deserved; he was only knighted in 2000. In later life he became a talented self-taught artist, brilliantly capturing the essence of arctic landscape and life.

NEIL ARMSTRONG 1930-2012

Things moved fast in the early days of space travel. The first primitive Russian sputnik orbited the Earth in 1957. Only four years later Yuri Gagarin became the first human to journey into outer space on 12 April 1961. Before this, it was uncertain whether the human body would continue to function properly when freed from gravity for the first time in its evolution, but during his single one-and-a-half hour orbit Gagarin showed that it was possible to eat, and to drink, when out of the earth's atmosphere.

On 20 April 1961 President Kennedy, nettled by the Russian lead in this important scientific field, wrote:

Do we have a chance of beating the Soviets by putting a laboratory in space, or by a trip around the moon, or by a rocket to land on the moon, or by a rocket to go to the moon and back with a man? Is there any other space program which promises dramatic results in which we could win? Are we working 24 hours a day on existing programs? If not, why not?

Less than 12 months later, John Glenn was to become the first American to reach orbit.

The first man to set foot on the moon, Neil Armstrong, had been a US Navy fighter pilot in the Korean War, then a test pilot, before becoming an astronaut. In 1966 he led the Gemini 8 space mission, which successfully completed the first-ever docking between two spacecraft. On 16 July 1969, the *Apollo 11* spacecraft left Cape Kennedy bound for the moon. On board were Armstrong, Buzz Aldrin and Michael Collins. Four days later, the astronauts passed behind the moon as seen from the earth, and while on its far side initiated rocket burns that would slow them down sufficiently to remain in lunar orbit, only 62 miles above the moon's surface.

Armstrong and Aldrin transferred to the lunar landing module, *Eagle*. Leaving Collins behind in the main spacecraft, the two men made their descent to the moon in just 12 minutes, landing on the surface of the Sea of Tranquility with only 30 seconds of fuel remaining. "Houston, Tranquility Base here. The *Eagle* has landed!" reported Armstrong. Six hours later, Armstrong finally made footfall on the lunar surface, uttering as he did so the famous line: "That's one small step for man, one giant leap for mankind." The moment was caught by cameras mounted on the side of the lunar module and seen by an estimated 500 million people worldwide.

Aldrin followed Armstrong down the ladder and both men spent some time collecting rock samples, setting up experiments and testing out various means of moving about in their restrictive spacesuits, before returning to *Eagle*.

There were five further missions to the moon but, in all, only

Armstrong: "one small step for man, one ginat leap for mankind"

12 people have ever set foot on it. The last two were Harrison Schmitt, a scientist, who amassed a large collection of rocks, travelling more than 20 miles in the Lunar Roving Vehicle to do so, and Eugene Cernan who, before he climbed back into the lunar module for the last time, left a plaque reading:

Here Man completed his first exploration of the Moon, December 1972 A.D. May the spirit of peace in which we came be reflected in the lives of all mankind.

After this the moon landings stopped, due to waning public interest and budgetary constraints. Humans have not left earth's orbit since.

JACQUES COUSTEAU 1910-1997

B orn in the village of Saint-Andre-de-Cubzac in southwestern France, Jacques Cousteau was only four when he learnt to swim. It was the beginning of a lifelong fascination with water and a career which would include co-inventing the Aqualung, pioneering marine conservation and, through his books and especially films, revealing the underwater world to an enthralled public. By bringing back stunning images and through his poetic interpretation of all he saw in the deeps, he transformed our view of the planet for ever. But it was a career which almost ended before it began. When he was 26, after graduating from the French naval academy at Brest and becoming a gunnery officer, he was involved in a near-fatal car accident.

As a result of this, Cousteau had to spend months swimming in the Mediterranean as therapy. To relieve the monotony, he was given a pair of small goggles worn by Japanese pearl divers and the wonders of the seabed, jungles full of colourful fish, were revealed to him. Soon after this, he met the inventor of a demand regulator, or cylinder, that fed cooking gas to cars in rationed, wartime France. He wondered if this device could instead deliver air to a diver. He experimented and, in 1943, produced the first SCUBA – a Self-Contained Underwater Breathing Apparatus. His experiments were often interrupted, however: during the war he worked for the French resistance, documenting troop movements, and after the war he helped the French navy clearing underwater mines.

A charismatic communicator, Cousteau was soon surrounded by people as enthusiastic as he was to explore the frontier he had opened. Little was known about the physiology of diving under pressure, of breathing compressed air, of human limits at depth, of embolisms and decompression sickness, and so early undersea exploration was fraught with unexpected hazards.

One of Cousteau's early passions was cinema and he was soon at work inventing waterproof cameras that would capture the beauty and wonder he was experiencing and make it available to a worldwide audience. *The Undersea World of Jacques Cousteau*, the first underwater documentary series, began in 1966 and continued for 30 years, providing armchair exploration for millions of television viewers worldwide. This led to a new kind of scientific communication, which he called "divulgationism", the interpretation of science intended for a general audience. Many in the scientific community frowned on this, but he ignored them, and popular science eventually became a mainstay in broadcast television.

His serious underwater exploration began in 1952 when the Guinness family gave him a converted Second World War minesweeper, the *Calypso*, which he refitted as a mobile laboratory for field research and used as his principal vessel for diving and filming. The first ever large-scale underwater archaeological expedition was to the Grand-Congloué islet near Marseille.

Capturing the wonders of the undersea world: Cousteau with his camera

Hundreds of terracotta amphorae were brought to the surface and the crew were the first to sip wine from the era of Aristotle. Soon afterwards, he was to predict, quite correctly, that porpoises had a kind of biological sonar system – known as echolocation. Observing a group of them accompanying his ship, he noticed that they appeared to know the optimal route through the Straits of Gibraltar, following his ship when he was on the right course but not when he deliberately veered a few degrees off it.

In 1954 Cousteau and the *Calypso* were commissioned to prospect in the Persian Gulf and discovered the first off-shore oil-bearing strata. In spite of – or perhaps because of – being in at the start of the global petroleum revolution, he always took an uncompromising stand against the hazards of oil pollution and nuclear waste. He was quick to see the threat to the Mediterranean from oil pollution and ill-managed coastal development, and was warning of the dangers of over-fishing, habitat destruction and global warming long before these issues became headline news. His warnings resulted in many international treaties, such as the Barcelona Convention in 1976, now signed by every country bordering the Mediterranean.

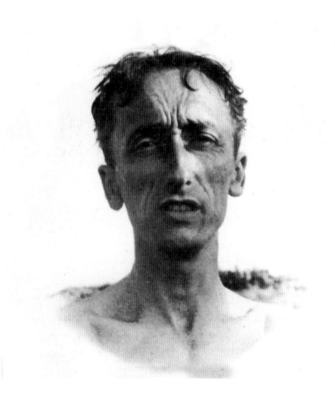

ROBERT BALLARD 1942-

An American ocean explorer, Robert Ballard has taken part in 120 underwater expeditions and logged more hours in the ocean deep than any other marine scientist. Using both manned and unmanned vehicles, he is best known for finding the wrecks of both the Titanic and the Bismarck, but it was his pioneering close-up studies of the great mid-oceanic ridge of volcanic mountains that circles the globe which have revolutionised scientific thinking. Indeed his expedition to the Galápagos Rift in 1977 overturned the conventional view of evolution.

The Galápagos Rift is a west to east spur of the Mid-Ocean Ridge in the Pacific Ocean, the largest underwater mountain range on Earth. Ballard and his team planned to investigate the volcanic and tectonic processes going on deep below the surface. There, molten magma flowing upwards from within the Earth creates the ridge, like a blister swollen with heat, which is dissipated through vents, or hot springs, into the surrounding ocean water.

On 16 February 1977 a manned submersible called *Alvin* descended 8,000ft – about a mile and a half – to the ocean floor. What Ballard and his team saw astonished them. Around a vent spewing out very hot water of up to 73C they found that the sea floor was teeming with life, most of it very strange and new to science. There were giant clams which, on being collected and brought to the surface, were found to have had their bodies taken over by billions of tiny bacteria. There were white crabs, small pink fish and clusters of vivid red-tipped tube worms, some almost 12ft long.

The scientists began to speculate about how the animals in these deep-sea oases got their energy and nutrients. Prior to this, all life on Earth was thought to be due ultimately to photosynthesis, in other words made possible by the energy of the sun. But here in the hot springs of the Galápagos Rift, in total darkness, life was thriving in far greater abundance than any previous theory could explain. Up to this point, it had been believed that life began in a shallow sunlit pool, a just-right environment stocked by chance with all the needed raw materials. From this comfortable cradle, it was supposed, the earliest microbes evolved to colonise other, harsher environments. According to this theory, life started at the surface and somehow made its way down to the volcanic deep-sea oases.

Suddenly, there was an alternative hypothesis. Could life have in fact begun in an early version of these vents, harnessing the energy of the *earth* not the sun to create a previously unknown carbon-based food chain? At these huge depths, where the sun's rays cannot reach, tiny bacteria appear to be using toxic hydrogen sulphide dissolved with the hot spring water, along with oxygen and carbon dioxide in the seawater, to replicate photosynthesis. Perhaps it was here that life on earth actually began.

Ballard's discovery has not only challenged conventional views about the origins of life but strongly affected the way scientists think about what life there might be elsewhere in the solar system and beyond.

MEG LOWMAN 1953-

Margaret Lowman, also known as Canopy Meg, is an American biologist, educator, ecologist, writer, explorer, and public speaker. She pioneered the science of canopy – essentially, the study of the upper branches of trees – and uses her research to inspire sustainability in the world's forests. She built the first canopy walkway in North America and for more than 30 years has designed hot-air balloons and walkways for treetop exploration to solve the mysteries of the world's forests, especially insect pests and ecosystem health. She works to map the canopy for biodiversity and to champion forest conservation around the world.

The uneven canopy layer of tropical rainforests is the home of unique flora and fauna not found in other layers of forests, some of which have evolved never to touch the ground. It is, perhaps, the richest environment on earth but one of the least studied, and the rapid destruction of rainforests everywhere makes research in

Dangling aloft... Lowman at work

this area particularly urgent. The canopy is just the top ten metres or so of a rainforest, but it intercepts 95 per cent of the sunlight, photosynthesising rapidly as a result, and so supports a mass of diverse life.

Lowman has been on innumerable expeditions to the canopy, accessing it in all sorts of ways, most of which involve climbing laboriously and dangerously up from the ground. In 1996, she went with a team to French Guiana, one of the last bastions of undisturbed tropical rainforest in South America, to access the pristine canopy in a remote spot by using a small hot-air balloon airship and raft above the treetops.

On this particular trip she also pioneered the use of a sled, or luge, a triangular inflatable structure with a netting floor, which is dangled below the airship and pulled through the canopy, rather like a motor boat towing a plankton-collecting device. She wore a harness, helmet, wasp-mask (in case of encountering an angry swarm) and her team stowed insect nets, beating trays, plastic bags, vials, marking pens, notebooks, clippers, aspirators, cameras, water and everything else they might need. Dangling aloft under the balloon, she and her team were able to sample nine canopy trees in an hour – something that without their new equipment would have taken several days to accomplish, using slingshots and ropes. Not only that, but they were able to sample the upper-most branches of the canopy as well as the slightly lower, more accessible ones. On returning to the ground, they had a wealth of material to examine.

Lowman's particular interest was herbivory (literally, plant eating), a phenomenon that creates a veritable pharmacy in the sky. Each species of plant produces its own unique chemical defence against being eaten, and in response many animals have adapted to store or sequester the toxic compounds, enabling them to feed on an otherwise poisonous leaf. The data Lowman acquired has changed the way ecologists view foliage.

At nights she would sleep in a large inflatable raft, which was lowered on to the top of the canopy to serve as a base camp. Sleeping under the stars, high above the forest and surrounded by such extreme diversity, was an extraordinary experience, though sometimes, when the rains came, it was wet and uncomfortable. Canopy research is not for the faint-hearted, but the rewards are immense – not least in giving a very real insight to the way plants survive, restricted as they are to one spot for their whole lives, and prey to every potential marauder that moves in and threatens to devour them.

CONCLUSION

The list of explorers covered in this book is far from comprehensive. I wish I had room for more. Edmund Hillary and Tenzing Norgay, for example, inspired the world when they became the first to reach the top of the highest mountain, Everest, even if, strictly speaking, they were not explorers. The exploits of lone yachtsmen and women also stir our imagination for their courageous feats on the mighty oceans but again, I feel, their adventures do not quite qualify as exploration.

There is still so much left to explore: it is thought that less than ten percent of the cave systems on earth have so far been discovered, and I would have liked to include one or two of the intrepid modern cavers who are revealing both natural beauty and biological secrets in their subterranean searches. Boundless life lies undiscovered beneath the sea – perhaps the greatest terrain for future research and discovery.

But it is not just caves, coral reefs and rainforests which contain infinite diversity. Our planet may now be well mapped, with no new lands left to discover, but within the known world there is still a wealth of creation to be revealed through arduous and often dangerous investigation.

Anyone who wants to become an explorer could do no better than consult the Royal Geographical Society. Their Geography Outdoors centre is there to help those planning expeditions. Originally called The Expedition Advisory Centre, it was set up by John Hemming and me after our Mulu expedition in Borneo. It has been run, brilliantly, ever since by one of my deputies on that expedition, Nigel Winser, who went on to become deputy Director of the RGS, and by his wife Shane Winser. See: https://www.rgs.org/in-the-field/advice-training

FURTHER READING

ANDERSON, J. R. L., The Ulysses Factor: the Exploring Instinct in Man (London, 1970).

BONINGTON, C., Quest for Adventure (London, 1981).

DELPAR, H. (ed.), The Discoverers: An Encyclopedia of Explorers and Exploration (New York, 1980).

FERNÁNDEZ-ARMESTO, F., The Times Atlas of World Exploration (London, 1991). GAVET-IMBERT, M. (ed.), The Guinness Book of Explorers and Exploration (Enfield, 1991).

GOODMAN, E., The Explorers of South America (New York, 1972).

HEMMING, J., The Conquest of the Incas (London, 1970).

HERBERT, W., The Noose of Laurels: The Discovery of the North Pole (London, 1989).

HOPKIRK, P., Trespassers on the Roof of the World (London, 1982).

KEAY, J., When Men and Mountains Meet (London, 1975).

KIRWAN, A. L. P., The White Road: A Survey of Polar Exploration (London, 1959). MIDDLETON, D., Victorian Lady Travellers (London, 1965).

MOORHEAD, A., The White Nile (London, 1962). The Blue Nile (London, 1962).

NEWBY, E., The World Atlas of Exploration (London, 1975).

——A Book of Travellers' Tales (London, 1985).

NOYCE, W. Springs of Adventure (London, 1958).

PARRY, J. H., The Discovery of the Sea (London, 1964).

PENNINGTON, P., The Great Explorers (London, 1979).

REID, A., Discovery and Exploration: A Concise History (London, 1980).

ROBINSON, J., The Oriental Adventure: Explorers of the East (New York and Boston, 1976),

URE, J., Trespassers on the Amazon (London, 1986).